Winning Strategies *for* Leaders

IRH Press

Originally published in Japan
as *Leader ni Okuru Hissho no Senryaku*
- Hito to Soshiki wo Ikashi, Atarashii Kachi wo Sozo seyo
by IRH Press Co., Ltd., in September 2008.

BOOKS

IRH PRESS
New York

ISBN: 978-1958655436

Cover Image: © HNK, fuku/PIXTA.jp, used under license.

Printed in Japan

First Edition

Winning Strategies *for* Leaders

How to Inspire People,
Maximize Team Potential,
and Create New Values

EL CANTARE
Ryuho Okawa

IRH Press

Contents

CHAPTER TWO

Clear and Deep Insight

—Freeing Yourself from Your Own Fixed Ideas

CHAPTER THREE

The Ability to Make Bold Decisions

—Being Thoughtful Without Being Indecisive

CHAPTER FOUR

An Unshakable Mind and an Indomitable Will

—The Moment Your True Worth Is Put to the Test

CHAPTER FIVE

Try to Be Fair and Selfless and Practice Love That Gives

—Virtue Is the Source of Trust

Words for Leaders 1

Part II

A Leader's Blind Spot

—Constantly Work on Your Foundations

CHAPTER SIX

Building the Foundations and Focusing on Your Strengths

CHAPTER SEVEN

Always Observe and Prepare for What Is Ahead

CHAPTER EIGHT

Building Up the Caliber to Withstand Adversities

CHAPTER NINE

Produce Positive Results by Using Your Personnel Effectively

Words for Leaders 2

Part III

An Innovator Who Keeps Creating Value

CHAPTER TEN

Fight According to the Size of Your Organization and Your Circumstances

CHAPTER ELEVEN

Providing Better Training for Your Employees

CHAPTER TWELVE

Gaining Support from the Invisible World

CHAPTER THIRTEEN

A Willingness to Contribute to Others and Society

Words for Leaders 3

EPILOGUE

*All chapters compiled in this book were originally recorded in Japanese and later translated in English.

Prologue

A Bird's-Eye View
—An Essential Quality for a Leader

Government-protected industries will perish one after another

In about 1991, it was widely reported that Japan's "bubble economy" had collapsed. However, what truly happened was not that the bubble economy collapsed, but rather that Japan's socialist system had begun to collapse. After the fall of the Soviet Union—the home of socialism—its effect had finally reached Japan. Although many Japanese scholars and media journalists, who were trained in Marxist economics, still say that the bubble economy burst at the time, that is not the correct interpretation. It was that Japanese socialism was beginning to collapse. It is now on the verge of total collapse (as of 2004).

If we understand this, the direction Japan is headed in is clear. It is the indoctrinated Marxist intellectuals and scholars who have no idea what will come in the future. They believe that Japan is supposed to be shifting toward socialism and communism, but now that they are seeing the fall of these political systems, they are unsure which direction Japan should now head in. They view Japan's current economic state through the lens of Marxist philosophy and therefore think that capitalism has collapsed, but because the reality is that socialism and communism have collapsed, they have no idea how the future will unfold. They are at a loss as to what to think.

What is truly happening is not the fall of capitalism, but rather, the fall of the socialism that has been prevailing in Japan. Nevertheless, it will take some time for Japanese socialism to collapse completely. It will likely take more time. However, once it collapses completely, a much freer world will unfold, where business transactions will be carried out with greater freedom.

Currently, more and more foreign capital is flowing into Japan, which is actually a good trend. On seeing this, some people may say that Japan is under foreign occupation or that it is suffering another defeat like it did in World War II. This is true in a sense, but the influx of foreign capital is telling Japan where it made mistakes in its ways of thinking. You could say that foreign capital is now flowing into Japan so that a true capitalist market economy can be established here. This notion allows us to foresee what is most likely to happen in the next 10 to 20 years. Japan will be moving in the direction I have just described.

For this reason, business owners must think independently from now on, rather than trying to rely on the government. Since the Edo Period (1603 - 1868), Japanese people have long had a tendency to rely on higher authorities, but those who retain this tendency will likely perish. Industries that depend on and expect government support and protection will perish one after another. Companies that are now monopolizing the market because they are receiving legal protection will also go out of business one after another. In the coming age, various protective measures will be abrogated, allowing companies to freely compete with one another. Only companies that are able to provide the best services and satisfy customer needs will survive, develop, and prosper. This is the kind of future I foresee.

Make efforts as you follow the macroscopic trend

Society is now in a period of transition. So, people need to carefully examine the direction that society is heading in. Otherwise, they could be swept away by the tides of change and suffer days of hellish difficulties, even though they may be good-hearted people.

Let me give you an example of what I mean by that. Suppose a man owns a small company with five employees. He runs his company in the best way possible, and all employees are working cheerfully, positively, happily, and are full of spirit. But what if he is unable to see the fundamental change in the social system that is taking place during this transition period? In no time at all, his company will be downgraded from an independent company to a subcontractor and then eventually will be forced to go out of business. As a result, all kinds of misfortune will befall the owner, such as having to flee from debt collectors in the middle of the night, his family being torn apart, having to file for divorce, and being unable to send his children to school. When he faces these hardships, he may want to curse God, as Job did in the Old Testament: "Why is this happening to me? I was working so hard." Unfortunately, all of this happened because he lacked another important ability—the ability to read the times.

Therefore, we must strive to read the times and look at the bigger picture, or in other words, we need to see the kind of world that God or Buddha—in the Western and Eastern sense, respectively—is planning to bring about. We will not be able to succeed unless we have this perspective and are limited to our own personal ideas. It is important to be aware of the macroscopic trajectory—God's or Buddha's Will regarding the direction society at large should move in—and make our own efforts in alignment with that trajectory.

I hope you will realize how important it is to develop the foresight needed to perceive this overall direction. Ask yourself how the world will change as you recognize the flow or the direction our age is heading in. This flow will bring about massive structural changes in society and create our future. You need to be aware of this and consider how to deal with it. It is essential to have a bird's-eye view and look at the trend over time from the perspectives of both the past and the future.

Part I

The Qualities of a Charismatic Leader

CHAPTER ONE

A Burning Sense of Mission

—Light the Flame of Enthusiasm Within You

1
How to Visualize an Ideal Future

Things appear differently depending on your mental state

The following story is an anecdote that is often told in business circles: Two employees from a trading company went to Africa to sell shoes. Upon seeing people in Africa walking barefoot, one of them sent a telex to the head office in Japan saying, "People here walk barefoot, so there's no market for shoes." On the other hand, the other employee sent a telex saying, "People here walk barefoot, so there is a potentially huge market if they adopt a shoe-wearing culture."

As this well-known, legendary anecdote shows, your interpretation of reality differs greatly depending on how you think of it. And the final outcome that you believe will manifest largely depends on whether or not you have a clear vision of the future.

When considering how you see your own visions, you probably do not think you have a biased view, but in reality, everyone wears their own tinted glasses through which they see the world. These tinted glasses reflect the color of their own mind. In other words, we are all looking at the world through a pair of glasses that are tinted in the color of our current mental state.

Visualize an ideal future and draw it toward you

Whenever you look at a person or a situation, you make your own judgments about them. But when that occurs, you must stop for a second and ask yourself, "How is my state of mind today? Is it good, fair, or bad compared to how my state of mind has been throughout the month?" If you find yourself in a bad state, you need to tell yourself, "Today, I am looking at things in a very negative way, so even if I feel pessimistic about what someone said, I will not take it that way. And if I happen to offend someone with my remarks, it's because of my negative thoughts, so I'll apologize as many times as necessary." You can control your mind by reminding yourself like this.

On the other hand, when you are in a good mood, you will be able to see decades into the future and talk about big ideas. In particular, if you have learned about the spiritual world, you may feel as though you can powerfully draw your vision of the future or big ideas into reality. You may feel as though you can draw ideas from ten or even a hundred years into the future toward yourself in the present. This can happen; it is just a matter of whether or not you can make it happen while you are still alive.

It is important to visualize an ideal future when you are in your best state of mind and believe you can bring it into reality. If you then make this reality happen two, three, four, or more times, you will develop this ability and become confident in bringing things into reality. After you successfully experience it three times, you will be able to believe that you can indeed make things happen.

The president of a well-known Japanese automobile company once boasted that his company's race car would win the next world motorsport competition. Not a single employee believed him at the time, but it turned out just as he said. His company won the Grand Prix and made a giant leap forward. The president's strong belief stuck firmly—like birdlime—to the vision that existed in the Real World* and brought it into this world. Even though all of the company's employees dismissed the idea as sheer folly, the strong belief of a single person—the president—brought it into reality. Companies with a top leader like that will definitely grow.

---

*The Real World refers to the other world or the Spirit World, where only thoughts exist and there are no material objects. It is a world where your thoughts manifest exactly as you imagine them; the moment you stop thinking about something, it disappears. When people in the earthly world hold a strong desire for something, it appears in the Real World exactly as they wish. It will then materialize in the earthly world depending on how earnestly they wish for it and how long they can sustain that wish.

2

Why Are You and Your Company Necessary?

Do you possess incredibly strong enthusiasm?

When we look at companies with abnormal growth after World War II, one thing stands out: they all have a CEO with incredibly strong enthusiasm. The level of their enthusiasm is nowhere near the average person's; it is completely different from that of a typical salaried worker. Salaried workers merely express enthusiasm in proportion to their salary, but CEOs of companies that make extraordinary development all have an extremely strong level of enthusiasm.

Where does such enthusiasm of a top leader come from? Needless to say, it comes from their sense of mission. Then, where does their sense of mission come from? It comes from their attitude of always seeking the answer to the question, "Why does our company exist?" An average CEO will answer, "I hope our company will last so that my employees can put food on the table and I can continue to work as the CEO," but this is not good enough. Even if you own a small company with only 30, 50, or 100 employees, it will surely grow larger if you, the CEO, are determined to become a light for the world or for society. Of course, there are many other conditions a company must satisfy in order to grow, but that will never happen unless the CEO has strong passion.

CEOs who constantly maintain exceptionally strong passion develop a centripetal force; they turn into magnets and change the people around them. This includes their employees, who will also turn into magnets and exert influence on their clients and even the company's competitors. As a result, the company will expand further.

Therefore, you need passion. Passion comes from a sense of duty toward your mission. You can awaken to this sense of duty by always seeking the answer to the questions, "Why does our company exist?" "Why should it keep existing?" "Why does society, the country, and the world need our company?" Business owners who keep thinking about these questions will develop strong belief, a sense of duty toward their mission, and passion.

Can you confidently say that your company is absolutely necessary?

To put it bluntly, it wouldn't matter that much if most companies were to disappear because there are tons of competitors. Some company owners may insist, "That's not true. We have a long tradition," "We've been in business for 100 years," or "We're a well-known company," but I think they are being tested to see whether or not they are really needed.

Let us take an automaker, Toyota, as an example. Although Toyota makes over a trillion yen (billions of US dollars) in profit annually, we would not be too troubled if it were to go out of business. Customers would simply shift to other automakers, which would allow underperforming competitors to rise. Knowing that this is the case, Toyota constantly practices *kaizen* (continuous improvement) to raise its level of quality.

Most people will not have a problem if a company or a shop closes down for good. Its employees may face difficulties for a while, but it is not such a big deal for other people. There are many other competitors, so the company can easily be replaced by another one. Consumers can easily buy TVs or cars from other companies. Clothes are also available at other stores. Even farm products can be purchased from other countries if they are not available in your own country. Therefore, you need to be able to answer why people should keep buying your products and why your company should continue to exist.

It is extremely difficult to make it so that your company is absolutely necessary. So, you must tell your employees to think of a product, service, or philosophy that makes them confidently say, "Our company is indispensable." This will nurture passionate employees, which will then lead to your company growing larger. There is a clear difference between companies with a philosophy and those without one. A sense of mission will arise in companies that have a CEO or a manager who keeps asking themselves the fundamental question, "Why is our company necessary?" So, please find your own answer to this question. As you seek the answer, you will clearly see what you need to do.

3

The Source of Energy for Companies That Enjoy Major Growth

The principle of management that can be learned from religion

There are many things we can learn from religion. What is it that people in business—company owners, managers, and business elites in particular—should learn?

The primary principle of management they should learn from religion is the concept of an ideal or belief. Religion is full of ideals and beliefs. Religion is an embodiment of an ideal that expresses how people or things should be. All religious activities are fundamentally aimed at creating Buddha Land, the Kingdom of God, a utopia, or an ideal world, depending on what it is called in each group. What is more, the believers who are striving to achieve their ideal are full of conviction. They believe, "What I'm doing is absolutely good," "This Truth is absolutely right," "I must achieve this goal at any cost," and they have a strong sense of mission that they carry out their activities with. People who devote themselves to religion have this characteristic.

I believe that this quality should also be incorporated into business activities, at least to some degree.

Konosuke Matsushita modeled his company on religion

There was a company owner who put this idea into practice—Konosuke Matsushita, the founder of Panasonic. He imitated religion and successfully incorporated religious thinking into his business activities. During the Showa Depression, which occurred before World War II, he visited a Japanese Shinto group called Tenrikyo. Upon seeing Tenrikyo full of vigor, he wondered, "Why is this religion so active and energetic when all businesses are struggling to survive?" He then realized that it was because they had an ideal and a sense of mission. He thought that the believers of Tenrikyo were convinced about what they had to do. They had a spirit of service and a sense of mission.

Thus, Matsushita modeled his company on religion, and we saw a company follow the example of religion. In the same way that religious founders formulate their basic teachings, the Panasonic founder came up with "Matsushita's Seven Principles" for his employees to follow. He thought that adopting this religious style of operation would enable him to run his company somewhat like a religion. Of course, most religious groups could not manufacture electrical appliances on their own, but Matsushita thought he could apply the principles and ways of thinking of religion to business management. He seemed to have opened his eyes to the secrets of management after observing Tenrikyo.

Think hard to establish your company's fundamental philosophy

A genuine ideal ignites a sense of mission in people. Therefore, you must develop a philosophy for your company that is similar to a religious ideal or mission. Think hard and think thoroughly about what you can accomplish through your business, or how your company can contribute to the creation of Buddha Land Utopia.

Economic principles also say that what is useless in the world will die out while what is useful to people will remain. That is why it is extremely important to think hard to establish your company's fundamental philosophy.

CHAPTER TWO

Clear and Deep Insight

–Freeing Yourself from Your Own Fixed Ideas

1

The Three Important Qualities Required of a Leader

A good sense of balance regarding money and people

I believe there are three important conditions that a person must satisfy to become a successful business owner. The first is to have a good sense of balance. This is required in two areas. The first area is finance. It is important for business owners to know how much income and expenditure their companies have. The second area is human resources. They must also be able to appoint the right personnel to the right position.

People can exert their full potential when they are assigned a role best suited to their abilities, but they cannot express their talents at all when assigned to an ill-suited job. For this reason, business owners need to have a good sense of balance when assigning positions to their employees. The bottom line is that they should be able to determine how best to allocate their personnel to increase the overall performance of the company.

An eye that sees through the past, present, and future

The second important condition is to be future-oriented. In other words, business owners should always be looking toward the future and anticipating what will happen in one, five, or ten years' time. It goes without saying that they should be looking ahead in their own business, but they must also think about how the world outside their industry is changing and how they will carry out their business in that kind of world in the future.

In fact, business owners need a perspective that sees through the past, present, and future. The perspective of the past refers to the view that the business owner had a year ago or at the time of founding the company. They need to reassess the current position, operation, and nature of their business from the past. At the same time, it is also important to view their business from the perspective of the future and think comprehensively about how they will develop and the amount of personnel, capital, and space they will need at a particular time in the future.

Then, how can you transcend the past, present, and future? To do this, I believe you need the ability to have a detached view of yourself. You cannot do this if you can only view yourself through your physical eyes. But once you are able to detach yourself from your physical body and view your past, present, and future objectively—as if you are looking at yourself from far up in the sky or from a third-person perspective—you should be able to transcend the past, present, and future. A leader must be able to look at themselves and their surroundings objectively without being absorbed by their own subjective feelings.

The willingness to give back to society

The third indispensable condition is having a constant desire to contribute to the world. Some people may become successful by pursuing only what benefits themselves or their companies, but in the long run, these people will definitely stumble at some point. This is not the kind of success you should aim for. I believe business owners should be willing to give back to society in one form or another. This attitude is what allows them to be in a privileged or advantageous position as a business owner. They must not forget this social perspective.

The second condition of a successful business owner is a "time-based" perspective, whereas this third condition is a "space-based" perspective. It is important for leaders to have the ability to look at themselves from this perspective, that is, within the context of their industry, society, or country.

2

An Eye for Both the Bigger Picture and the Small Details

Constantly develop your ability to see the bigger picture

People who are not able to see the bigger picture, or who lack a macro-level view, are not very suited to become business owners. Suppose a man happens to possess a specialized skill that helps him develop a product that becomes a big hit. He may then take his work beyond a personal level and commercialize it by setting up a company. But once he establishes a company, he will have new issues to deal with—management issues—and unfortunately, he will not be able to run his company successfully just by focusing on his specialized skill.

Once you launch a business, you need to have a broad perspective and the ability to see the bigger picture. You should always have a comprehensive view of what is going on in your company, in the market, in the domestic economy, in the global economy, and in politics as a whole. You also need to observe where society is headed and constantly develop your ability to see the bigger picture. To do this, you need to keep collecting new information about what is going on outside your company. Moreover, you should think on a scale much greater than your employees. A business owner needs to think about the company's overall situation, its external affairs, and its future, even though the employees may be preoccupied with the work at hand. This is an indispensable quality of a business owner.

A business owner should put their heart into developing the ability to see the bigger picture because it is an essential ability for leading a large number of people. It is largely an innate ability, but even an innate ability will not shine unless it is polished. So, you must remind yourself of the need to constantly develop your ability to see the bigger picture.

Find new opportunities for the future in the smaller details

Having said this, you will not succeed as a business owner if you only focus on seeing the bigger picture. As you grasp the whole picture, you must also pay attention to the smaller details because those are where you will find new opportunities that lead you to a brighter future.

Nowadays, you often hear about a "hands-on approach" to company management. When a CEO occasionally drops by to inspect their company's factory or local store, they may see something that the people working there do not. Contrary to the CEO's expectations, the factory or local store might be a complete disaster.

Let us take a supermarket as an example. CEOs and executives of nationwide supermarket chains usually make decisions based on reports, but sometimes, when they visit one of their stores, they may find something completely unexpected. For instance, they may find a completely different floor layout from before or totally different items on the shelves, incompetent cashiers who are unable to provide appropriate service, disloyal employees who do not try to resolve customer complaints, and other noisy workers who are busy chatting instead of listening to their customers. There was even a case where a store moved its best-selling products to the back of the shelf and placed the slow-moving inventory in the front instead. When the CEO asked why, the store employees said they did so because they wanted to avoid accumulating excess stock of unpopular products. The CEO quickly saw this as a big problem. Sure enough, their customers would complain that the store displayed products they did not need in the front while hiding what they needed in the back.

Therefore, while it is important to have a grasp of the overall operation of the company, it is just as important to pay attention to the small details. The owner of a supermarket chain, for example, needs to be aware of what is going on in the stores, the size of each store, the products they are selling, how the products are being sold, the attitude of the store clerks, and even the reactions of their customers. By paying attention to each and every complaint from their customers, they will be able to do better in the future. Sometimes, the small details can have an effect on the overall management of a company. A small discovery in one place may be applicable to other situations as well.

The secret to running a company successfully

In the process of developing the right mindset to successfully run a company, business owners must always strive to see the bigger picture first. They need to study many things in order to think about their grand strategy, the trends of the times, the future, and the company or industry as a whole. They have to read books and newspapers and watch the news, so they should always be busy studying.

At the same time, they must also pay attention to the small details. However, just as grasping the bigger picture alone is not enough, just focusing on the small details will not be enough either. Those who are preoccupied with the small details tend to lack the ability to see the bigger picture. Therefore, you need both abilities.

How should you go about developing both of these abilities? This is the ultimate test of a business owner's ability to "steer the ship." It is essential to keep honing your ability to both grasp the bigger picture and pay attention to the small details.

3

Once You Visualize a Dream, Turn It into Cash

Can you talk about your dreams?

Business owners, or business executives, need to be dreamers. People without ideals or dreams that they can talk about passionately are not suited to become business owners. Of course, some people may be quick to retort that you cannot run a company without understanding reality. That is, indeed, true. You need to have an outstanding practical ability. However, it will be very difficult to fulfill your work as a business owner in the truest sense if that is all you can do. This is because owners are entrusted with the future of many people. Tens, hundreds, or even more people stake their lives on the ideas, policies, or potential of business owners as they come to take part in their businesses. So, owners need to guide them into the future. Just as Moses led the Israelites out of Egypt and directed them toward Canaan, business owners need to lead people in the right direction and demonstrate exceptional leadership.

Therefore, you should first ask yourself whether you have the ability to talk about your dreams, ideals, or grand visions. Calmly reflect on your mind and try to visualize what you must do. Do you see a clear image of what you must do? Are you able to motivate yourself to achieve your dreams without being directed or instructed by someone else? You must find the answers to these questions by yourself. Unless you are able to map out a future vision for yourself, talk about your dreams, and motivate yourself, you do not have what it takes to become a business owner. But even if you do not have these abilities and are only good at administrative work, you can still be an excellent manager. I would advise these people to find work under someone with a grand vision and assist him or her.

No matter how small a company may be, the owner is still the head. So, please be sure to come up with a dream and have the aspiration to realize it.

The ability to make your dream come true

Once you come up with a dream, please also engrave deeply into your heart that a dream requires realistic support and a solid foundation. What I mean by this is money. You cannot run a company without a good sense of money and finance.

Maintaining a business requires large amounts of capital. It requires more than a single person can earn alone. Operating factories and offices, hiring employees, and paying their salaries certainly call for tremendous amounts of income and result in large expenses. Unless you can understand and think in terms of cash flow, your dream will not be realized. Therefore, in addition to the ability to visualize your dream, you need the ability to realize the cash needed to make your dream come true. This means you need to be able to draw up a financial plan for your business and execute it using your own efforts or with the support of others.

CHAPTER THREE

The Ability to Make Bold Decisions

—Being Thoughtful Without Being Indecisive

1
A Common Trait of Leaders Who Bring About Their Own Demise

The battle between Song and Chu

About 2,600 years ago, during the Spring and Autumn period in ancient China (an era slightly before Confucius and partly overlapping Shakyamuni Buddha), many small states appeared and fought each other for hegemony. One of them was Song, which was led by Xiang Gong, also known as Duke Xiang. He is known for the expression, "Song Xiang (Duke Xiang)'s benevolence," which has led to a controversial topic of discussion about benevolence and righteousness.

One day, Duke Xiang of Song harbored an ambition to rule the world and decided to fight for hegemony. He was successful until he faced a battle with the neighboring state of Chu. The Chu army, which was overwhelmingly large compared to the small Song army, was crossing the river to attack Song. So Duke Xiang's counselor advised him, "Attack them now, or you won't stand a chance." But Duke Xiang dismissed the advice and said that attacking the enemy while they are crossing the river goes against his sense of benevolence and righteousness. Then, when the counselor saw the entire Chu army finish crossing the river, he advised Duke Xiang, for the second time, to attack them now. But once again, Duke Xiang refused to give the green light. He said, "They've just crossed the river and aren't in formation yet. Attacking them now would go against propriety and be considered a shameful act as a warrior. I don't think taking advantage of the enemy's weakness is a graceful act."

Duke Xiang finally launched his attack when the enemy was fully prepared, only to be badly beaten and lose many of his soldiers. His army was routed, and he, too, fled for his life. An injury to his groin eventually led to his death.

What was lacking in Duke Xiang?

This anecdote is often referred to as "Song Xiang's benevolence," which gave rise to divided opinions among people of later generations. Confucianists and others who have studied the teachings of Confucius evaluate Song Xiang positively and say, "If Song Xiang was not a man of benevolence, then who is?" On the other hand, those who value military strategies or are referred to as legalists criticize him and say, "Song Xiang was not a man of benevolence—he was a fool. He put his army in jeopardy and even suffered a fatal wound himself. How could you call that benevolence?"

Perhaps Duke Xiang was rather a religious person. Had he pursued the path of religion, he would have made a successful religious leader, but because he was the ruler of a state, he brought this kind of tragedy on his people. His approach would have made sense if he were confronting a much smaller enemy. But sadly, he was confronting a large enemy when he only had a small army. Anyone could see that he would lose if he fought a large army head-on. I can only think that he lacked wisdom; he harbored an ambition to conquer the world, but engaged in an act of benevolence toward the enemy despite having a small army. He certainly was benevolent, but he did not have sufficient wisdom. Duke Xiang was indeed considerate and kind and was admired by future generations, but his lack of wisdom led to his demise and drove his army into near annihilation. This is an extremely difficult part of being a leader—knowing when to be benevolent and when to be wise.

The weakness of an extreme idealist

You may probably think of this story as someone else's problem, or merely an anecdote from 2,600 years ago. But the reality is that everyone experiences a similar thing every day. Many people have a habit of saying things that put them at a disadvantage. If someone like this is a sales manager, for example, he may have a slip of the tongue and say to his client, "To tell you the truth, we're at risk of bankruptcy next month, so we would be grateful if you could do business with us." This kind of remark will only blow his chances because, on hearing it, the client will probably turn down the deal. Things like this happen often.

People with a religious disposition may have a good character, but they tend to be too soft and can miss opportunities in the way I have just described. If you think you are one of them, please be aware of it. It may not be much of an issue if you are the only one involved, but depending on the situation, it could cause trouble for many people. If that is the case, you need to change the way you think.

In modern society, people who have qualities that resemble Song Xiang's benevolence tend to support the idea of unarmed neutrality. They may insist that a country should remain unarmed and simply endure whatever comes, even if they are under a nuclear threat. They are idealists, no doubt, but the way they think is so extreme that they are essentially useless when a crisis occurs.

2

The Two Weapons to Sharpen Your Decision-Making Ability and Produce Good Results

Knowledge-based management increases the total amount of wealth

Various things can be considered business resources; iron ore, coal, petroleum, and natural gas are examples of physical resources. However, if you were to ask me the most important resource in the present age and the ages to come, without hesitation, I would reply that it is knowledge. There can be no doubt on that score. Knowledge is the only resource that has been used continuously. Its use will continue to increase steadily. Knowledge is an inexhaustible storehouse of new resources for businesses. Moreover, it is a resource that can expand and be recycled. In other words, new knowledge can give birth to new resources and new results, which in turn will give birth to more new knowledge.

In line with modern management theory, we now know that overall wealth can be increased through skillful management. This was a key discovery made about two centuries ago. If each person is working separately, we cannot expect to see more production than the aggregate labor input. On the other hand, if all of the workers pool their knowledge and wisdom and do their own jobs well, it is possible to create wealth greater than what would be created if they had all worked separately. This is the hallmark of modern industrial society. For example, if an individual were to try producing steel from iron ore, he would not be able to produce much on his own, nor would he be able to turn the steel into something usable. However, if there is capital available to form a corporation, hire many workers, and establish a division of labor, large volumes of products can be produced. Those products will be markedly superior to any steel products that an individual could make on their own. The revenue from such an organized operation would be much larger as well. By increasing the overall level of wealth in this way, we can also greatly increase the affluence of each individual.

All of this has become possible thanks to management systems that enabled factories to be built and products to be manufactured that were then distributed through domestic and overseas sales routes. In addition, management systems have allowed large amounts of raw materials to be imported cheaply from foreign countries. It is therefore fair to say that intellectual endeavors are the foundation of all of this.

Knowledge-based management does not refer solely to knowledge that you currently possess or your current level of intelligence. Knowledge that is used as a business resource can expand limitlessly into the future. Unless you are always striving to learn, you will fall behind in a year's time. This holds true for individuals, as it does for organizations. New things are constantly being created all around you.

Time-based management maximizes output

Time is a limited resource. Each person has only 24 hours in a day, and even if you add up all the time available to an organization, it will not exceed the amount available to the total number of its members. However, every business that has great potential for development focuses on shortening the amount of time it takes to do something. Shortening time can foster business development. For example, it is a fact that Japan's GDP (gross domestic product) has grown tremendously since the advent of the *Shinkansen* (bullet train). The reason is that it has allowed an individual to accomplish a lot more in a day. The nation's GDP has expanded as the time spent on transportation has greatly decreased compared to the time spent in the past, when people had to travel on foot or take overnight sleeper trains on the Tokaido Line.

Another example is seasonal products. For instance, if summer merchandise is only produced once during the summer, then the other seasons of the year will be unproductive blanks.

One way to think is that summer merchandise can only be produced or sold during the summer, but in fact, there are some summer goods that can also be produced during winter. For example, you might have the impression that ice cream is something that can only be produced in summer, when in fact it can be produced just as well in winter and then stored. There are many examples like this.

If things are examined from a time-saving perspective, all kinds of changes can be made. How can you go about reducing the amount of time spent on something? How can you speed up your work? How can you advance the schedule for achieving the next set of results? Asking these questions is an important part of producing good results. An unresolved problem will hinder you from taking on the next task, but by reducing the amount of time required to resolve each issue, you can take on the next task faster.

The ultimate in time-based management can be expressed in the proverb, "Each day has enough trouble of its own" (Matthew 6:34). There is also a Japanese phrase that says, "Live each day as if it were the last." In short, it is important to do everything you can on any given day. This is a very important attitude. Some people may say, "I won't work until the time is right" or "Due to other circumstances, I'll skip doing this today," but this attitude goes against the spirit of time-based management.

It is important to think about what you can do to reduce the time involved or how you can shorten the time needed to do something. Decreasing the amount of time involved simultaneously creates time that you can use for other things. For instance, it may take you three hours to go to a particular destination by bullet train, but it will just take an hour if you travel by air. That will free up two hours, giving you two additional hours for other things.

How to make quick decisions

Time-based management also means making quicker decisions. As an organization becomes larger, the number of echelons of management within it will increase, which inevitably results in a delay in decision-making and information flow. Modern companies are all struggling to come up with ways to streamline the process and shorten the time it takes to accomplish a goal. To reduce time, they use many convenient tools such as telephones and fax machines.

Compared to the past, the amount of time available to us has increased, despite the fact that human life spans remain the same. We have managed to create more usable time by eliminating unnecessary procedures.

All rapidly growing enterprises and venture businesses today use time-based management and think about how to speed up their work. In the past, for example, documents would often be piled up in the CEO's inbox for three days or a week, waiting for his approval. And what was the CEO doing all that time? Playing golf! Now, however, it is normal for companies to focus on how to make quicker decisions. In fact, the trend now is to get rid of managerial approval altogether. The days when approval was needed from 20 to 30 executives are long gone and, instead, the emphasis is now placed on delegating decisions to the people near the frontline.

3

Overcoming Indecisiveness

People with leadership skills are quick decision-makers

One of the important requirements of a leader is the ability to make good decisions. An outstanding leader is always an excellent decision maker, and there are no exceptions to this. If you are unable to make decisions and take action when necessary, you will miss out on a large portion of life's treasures that you could otherwise have been able to enjoy. By considering every possibility and taking too much time before making a decision, you may miss the chance of a lifetime. Those who hold leadership positions should be capable of making quick decisions. This means they need to have a superior ability to foresee the future.

Making quick decisions does not simply mean choosing between left and right; it involves the ability to instantly think of the best way to proceed amid ever-changing circumstances and the march of time. It also entails the ability to correct your decisions right away when they turn out to be wrong. In this way, the ability to make good decisions is synonymous with thoughtfulness, although too much thoughtfulness can make people become indecisive.

The source of the ability to make decisions

A true decision-making ability means having the judgment to solve complicated problems from a broader perspective. It also means having the ability to deal with practical day-to-day problems at work or in life based on careful observation of circumstances, which requires constant adjustments to decisions already made.

In terms of decision-making, the greater a person is, the more quickly they will admit their errors. Being a good decision-maker does not mean never changing a decision you have made or being stubborn. Good leaders follow through on their convictions, but they are also prepared to examine whether they are acting for their own benefit out of selfish desires or whether they are working for the benefit of many people in accordance with God's Will.

The source of the ability to make decisions is the love of many people. This means leaders must sometimes make decisions that are disadvantageous to themselves. When they find that they have taken a wrong action or made a wrong decision, they need to admit it outright. You, too, may sometimes find it hard to admit your faults or mistakes out of pride. Everyone makes inappropriate remarks that hurt others or makes a slip of the tongue at times. When this happens, do not let your pride get in the way or be preoccupied with how to protect your small ego. Instead, have the courage to change your decision for the sake of many people. This attitude will generate more power to make your next decision.

The two necessary perspectives to attain great success

There are two important attitudes to a successful life: first, an iron will that allows you to overcome any difficulty, and second, a flexibility that enables you to adjust your attitude as you carefully analyze different circumstances. Without flexibility, you cannot hope to achieve success.

Many of those who have achieved great success have possessed both of these attitudes. If you wish to achieve great success in a decades-long life, both of these attitudes—sticking to your convictions and making decisions from a broad perspective, and being flexible and constantly changing yourself from a day-to-day perspective—are indispensable.

CHAPTER FOUR

An Unshakable Mind and an Indomitable Will

–The Moment Your True Worth Is Put to the Test

1
Expand Your Scope of Responsibility

How to measure your stature

A person's stature is determined by the scope of responsibility that he or she takes on. There are a variety of criteria that can be used to measure a person's stature, and the willingness to take responsibility is one of them. In other words, if you want to know what kind of person you are, what position you occupy in society, and what your stature is, then you simply need to consider the extent to which you are prepared to take on responsibility. This is an extremely important point because people are usually less willing to do this than they care to admit.

Taking responsibility—not only for your own life, but also for the lives of others—is the vital quality required of a leader. The number of people you are willing to take responsibility for shows whether or not you possess the stature of a leader. People who have an irresponsible leader will have difficult lives indeed.

Responsibility eventually develops into love

When it comes to taking responsibility, you must first look at your own situation in a totally honest way. If you feel you have failed at what you have been doing, then you must admit that it is your responsibility. Only then will you find the step to take next. However, if instead you try to place the blame on the people around you or on external conditions, then you will never be able to improve yourself. The ability to admit to a mistake, even if it puts you in a disadvantageous position, is indispensable in allowing you to develop a powerful spirit of independence.

When experiencing a failure, it is only natural not to want to take responsibility for it and instead to try to blame all sorts of external factors. Actually, there is a good reason for doing this. If you analyze the causes of failure, you will find that the fault does not lie in just one person; everyone involved has a share of the blame. That is why people like to comfort themselves by saying that a mistake is the result of various external factors and use them in their defense. This is quite a natural reaction. Unless you think in this way, a failure may make you very nervous and cause you to worry endlessly, which could keep you from ever getting back up again.

Nevertheless, we are usually impressed by people who feel a level of responsibility that is beyond their duty. We find these people quite exceptional. But while it is easy to apply this to someone else, it is very difficult for us to apply it to ourselves. So I would like you all to try to make the effort to become a person like this.

It is usually clear whether or not you have done something that has directly caused a problem, so sometimes you can be exempt from taking primary responsibility. However, there is such a thing as "indirect responsibility."

Let me take an example of a mother whose son falls while playing in a park with his friend. She may only be able to think of blaming her son's friend, but there is another way of looking at this situation. She could think that she is also at fault because she was not aware of the potential danger that existed. By thinking like this, she can take greater responsibility. If the mother thinks to herself, "It is my fault that my son fell. I took too long shopping today, and that's when the accident occurred," she can avoid blaming others. When you admit that you share the responsibility for what happened, you will no longer feel like blaming others.

Therefore, make an effort to enlarge the extent of the responsibility you are prepared to take. As you continue with this discipline, what you thought of initially as responsibility will eventually be transformed into love. This is guaranteed to happen.

2

Remain Unshaken During a Losing Streak by Grasping the Bigger Picture

Viewing wins and losses from an overall perspective

There is a viewpoint that goes even further than just the idea of winning versus losing in life. It focuses on a way of not suffering complete defeat. When failures keep coming, and you are facing imminent defeat, focus on what you can win to avoid losing completely. This is a defense-based viewpoint—looking at what you can win to avoid complete failure. Find the area that enables you to avoid complete defeat even if you fail elsewhere.

There is yet another approach that uses more positive thinking. With this approach, you focus on what is required to achieve overall victory. If you can win at the key point that guarantees your overall victory even at the cost of small defeats, then you can ignore everything else.

Consider focusing on these two viewpoints I have just described. We are prone to think about winning at everything versus losing at everything, but that is not what usually happens in reality. So, do not think in terms of all or nothing. Instead, think about how to achieve overall victory even at the cost of some defeats. This is one approach you could consider taking. So, think of what to abandon in order to succeed as a whole, and find what needs to be done to do so. Alternatively, find the one area that will lead you to avoid complete defeat, even if you suffer small defeats. The point is to have a bird's-eye view, or an understanding of victories and defeats as viewed from the overall situation.

The type of leader that subordinates can trust and follow

Seeing from a broad perspective is indeed very difficult. But to achieve great success in your life and be a leader of others, you definitely need to cultivate this perspective.

When subordinates come to their leader to report their failures, they will not be as shaken if their leader has a broader perspective and does not regard their failures as an overall defeat. The subordinates will not become nervous as long as the leader clearly understands what level of failure they can afford without suffering complete defeat, or the minimum level of success that is needed to ensure overall victory.

If the leader remains unshaken in this way, other people, who would otherwise react nervously to each victory or defeat, will also become calmer. Subordinates often panic because they do not know whether something that happens means victory or defeat for them. That is why their emotions sway back and forth with each small outcome. But they will be relieved when their leader distinguishes victory from defeat and calmly watches the events unfold from a broad perspective. Actually, they will relax and just wait to receive the leader's judgment. If the leader says it is not a defeat, they will trust that it is not a defeat. If the leader says it is a victory, they will trust that it is a victory. They will leave this judgment up to their leader and will be able to concentrate on their own work.

However, it is often difficult to see what small victories and small defeats mean from a broader perspective, so some leaders make judgments based on trivial matters. Under a leader like this, subordinates will look at small failures as total defeat, and may all run away. This is the difficult part. It is similar to an army that retreats at the sound of waterfowl wings flapping. Indeed, everyone has a lot of fear, so it is natural that they feel like running away even at a slight sign of defeat. At times like that, whether or not the leader has the ability to see the big picture makes a significant difference.

3
Learning from History

Kaishu Katsu took his enemy by surprise by appearing unarmed

Wisdom can bring forth extraordinary success, but there is one thing I want to add, which is, "There are times when you run out of wisdom. When that happens, you need to demonstrate courage."

These are the words of Japanese statesman Kaishu Katsu (1823 - 1899). Throughout his life, Kaishu Katsu faced many battles of life or death. There were times when he had wise ideas and other times when he did not. It requires wisdom to constantly be the winner, but there are, of course, times when you run out of wisdom. When you run out of strategies and have no way out, you need to use courage to win. In the end, courage can be the deciding factor in a battle.

It is said that there were over 20 assassination attempts made on Kaishu Katsu. There were not many ways to survive assassination attempts in his time; assassination units were always roaming around, and many of them were going after Kaishu's life. When an individual is targeted by assassins, having many guards may be of no use. No matter how hard you try to protect yourself by hiring security guards, when you fall, you fall, much like Kozukenosuke Kira in the Japanese historical tale, *The 47 Ronin*.

When an assassin appeared at his house, Kaishu Katsu greeted him unarmed, which left the killer dumbfounded. To Kaishu, he was just another assassin, so he appeared in a red lounge robe, calm and composed. It could have been one of his strategies to catch the assassin by surprise. Because Kaishu appeared as an unarmed, kind old man, the killer hesitated to slay him. Kaishu then welcomed the assassin into his house and eloquently talked about international affairs as he showed him a globe of the world. By the time they were done talking, the assassin completely lost the will to kill Kaishu and left without carrying out what he had originally intended to do. People say that Ryoma Sakamoto was another man who went after Kaishu's life but ended up becoming his pupil.

Why Yoshinobu Tokugawa fell

Today, there is a debate over whether Yoshinobu Tokugawa, the last leader of the Tokugawa Shogunate (military government), was an outstanding figure or not. Some people say that he was the greatest leader since Ieyasu Tokugawa, the founder of the Tokugawa Shogunate, or that he was the second coming of Ieyasu. But I have the impression that he relied too heavily on his intellect and lacked courage. Strongly influenced by the Mito school of thought, which advocated reverence for the emperor, he had such high reverence for the emperor that he could not confront an enemy if they fought for the emperor. He was highly intelligent and had learned to deeply respect the emperor. Because of this, he was completely powerless against an enemy who stood on the side of the imperial family.

In retrospect, it was probably good that he was defeated. Nevertheless, I think Yoshinobu could have come up with other ways to win. At the very least, given the large size of his military and the advantage that this gave him, had he been an outstanding leader, he would have been able to win in any number of ways. In the end, I think he lacked courage.

As the saying "Hoist with his own petard" goes, intelligent people sometimes fail because they are overconfident in their intellect or because their intellect keeps them from succeeding. Once you have racked your brain and used all the knowledge and wisdom that is available to you, the only resources you can resort to are your physical and mental strength. Although wisdom can generate hundreds, thousands, or even tens of thousands of times more power than physical strength can, it can also run out. As Kaishu Katsu said, when that happens, you need to be courageous. You need to convince yourself to use courage as your last resort.

What to do when you have made the wrong decision

There are times when we must make critical, life-or-death decisions in our personal relationships as well as in business transactions involving investments, new strategies, or overseas expansion. When it comes to venturing into an unknown world or field, it can be hard to know what to do, no matter how much research or investigation has been done; sometimes, no amount of information or contemplation will be enough. Even so, that is not a valid excuse. You have to make a decision even if it turns out to be wrong later on. This is especially true for top executives.

In the end, it all comes down to whether or not you have courage. Even if you make the wrong decision, you can try to get back on the right track as soon as you realize you have made a mistake. You will not even know that you have made the wrong judgment unless you take action. You will never realize it as long as you keep putting off making a decision. Once you realize you have made a mistake, the next step is clear—all you need to do is come up with a new strategy, whether it is to retreat or find another way to achieve your goal. To sum up, wisdom can run out, so in the end, it all comes down to courage.

CHAPTER FIVE

Try to Be Fair and Selfless and Practice Love That Gives

—Virtue Is the Source of Trust

1

No Reflection, No Growth

The common trait of people and companies that go under

You may experience many failures in managing a business, so it is crucial that you reflect on them, one by one. Incompetent people, whether or not they are business executives, blame everything on external factors. They blame their failures on others, such as the government, their industry, a foreign country, or a rising new competitor. People with this tendency typically fail, and so do companies.

Companies that go bankrupt always blame others and the environment. In times of deflation, they blame deflation, and in times of inflation, they blame inflation. In economic stagnation, when there is neither inflation nor deflation, they blame the stagnant economy. By doing so, they try to avoid taking responsibility. However, under the same circumstances, some businesses will flourish while others will decline, and there must be a reason for this. Companies that do not reflect on themselves have no chance of further development.

Some companies grow even during a recession

All companies, without exception, have weaknesses—there is not a single company without one. But because they have strengths that make up for their weaknesses, they are able to survive; their strengths either offset or outweigh their weaknesses. However, if you want to grow your business further, you must reflect on the weaknesses of your company. Examine your company and find anything that is a weakness from your viewpoint. Have your employees rack their brains to find the company's weaknesses. Then, you must all try to evaluate your company from the perspective of your customers.

When your company's products stop selling, for example, you might think it is because the income of your customers has decreased due to deflation. Even so, it is unlikely that your competitors throughout the country are all experiencing a similar decline in sales. People will still buy what they need, even if their income drops. This is only natural. They still need shelter, food, and clothing—so they will keep buying the necessities. However, when they have less money to spend, they become more selective about what they buy. They stop buying low-quality or low-value items, and instead, go to places that sell higher-quality products at better prices. It is as simple as that. Therefore, you cannot blame external factors for your company's decline unless those factors also cause all of your competitors to go out of business.

Imagine that a business goes bankrupt during a recession. You cannot fully blame the recession because there are other businesses that continue to grow during that time. If a supermarket goes out of business, for instance, people may say it is because of a recession, but that is not always the case. Perhaps it went out of business because other supermarket stores were steadily expanding. This is indeed difficult to accept for the owner who files for bankruptcy. The owner will probably have loved their store, been proud of it, and perhaps even been arrogant. They probably felt confident and satisfied. Because of this, they may not have been able to admit to the faults, weaknesses, or failures of their company. However, your business will not survive unless you acknowledge your company's weaknesses. If you don't, in times of failure, all you will be able to do is sit by and watch everything crumble. Therefore, the teaching of self-reflection is extremely important, particularly in business management.

Asahi Breweries: the secret behind their recovery

Self-reflection is a discipline that you must do yourself in your own company. Other companies will not be so kind as to tell you how your company can improve. Do you think your competitors will tell you your company's flaws? They most certainly will not because doing so will help your company recover. Instead, they will simply watch and wait quietly for your company to go under and then gloat about it. They will think to themselves, "His company will go out of business in three years. When it does, we can take over his customers." People will never give their competitors advice about how to improve their business. Someone who does this is overly nice and will lose. A person like that is bound to lose in business.

Let me use the Japanese beer company, Asahi Breweries, as an example. They had been in decline, but after producing a new product called Asahi Super Dry, they made a comeback, eventually catching up to their rival, Kirin Brewery, giving them a hard time. Currently, Asahi and Kirin are competing for the top position in the Japanese beer industry. Here is a well-known story: Asahi Breweries, which had been struggling at the time, appointed a new CEO from the banking sector rather than the beer industry. The former vice president of a bank became the new CEO of Asahi Breweries. Because he knew nothing about beer, he visited other beer companies and humbly and politely asked them to teach him about beer. He learned about how to sell beer better and also about the weaknesses of his own company. As a result, the CEO discovered that his company had been neglecting to recall stale beer from retail stores. Beer loses its flavor over time, so it does not taste good after a while. Having learned about this weakness, the CEO instructed his employees to collect and dispose of all old beer. He then researched the kind of beer customers want by consulting people from other beer companies. Eventually, Asahi Breweries developed and launched its new brand called Super Dry. Ironically, the beer companies that kindly gave him advice all lost to Asahi.

This would come as a shock. This is exactly why your competitors rarely give you advice or information that might help you do better in your business. In most cases, they just wait for you to go bankrupt without saying a word. However, if you approach them humbly, just as the new CEO of Asahi Breweries did, they might teach you some important lessons. This is one of the secret techniques to doing well in business.

2
The Timeless Virtue of Lincoln

Why Lincoln was able to unite America

Abraham Lincoln became the president of the United States at the dawn of the Civil War, when the country was on the verge of division. The U.S. remains a single nation today thanks to Lincoln's firm determination to keep America united. This is why Lincoln is still respected to this day.

Back in Lincoln's time, people in the South had their own reasons to keep slaves. The Southerners ran many large farms, which required cheap labor. That is why many people from Africa were brought over as slaves to do various kinds of work, such as cultivating cotton, and were treated like livestock. Slaves were considered property by the people in the South. So, Lincoln's address to free black slaves was seen as a violation of property rights that the Southerners could not accept. Treating black slaves on a par with white people meant the Southerners would have to pay them accordingly, which would rapidly reduce their productivity and lead to the poor operation of their farms. People in the North were mostly against slavery because they did not own many slaves, but in the South, people were fully in support of slavery. For them, it was a fight to protect their property.

As history shows, the Civil War broke out to prevent America from splitting into two. Ultimately, the Union in the North came out victorious, thereby preserving America as a single unified nation. The president at the time was Abraham Lincoln. Lincoln's motto was, "With malice toward none." It is a wonder how someone with this motto was able to lead the nation through the Civil War. Lincoln was by no means a man of unparalleled bravery or unmatched valor. Contrary to what people may expect, he was not a man with an excellent decision-making ability or a combative spirit, like the Japanese warlord Nobunaga Oda.

A leader stands alone and can only pray

The following anecdote has been passed down about Lincoln. A friend of Lincoln's once stayed over at the White House. He woke up in the middle of the night to use the restroom, and as he walked down the corridor, he heard a deep groan. Wondering what it could be, he walked toward the deep groan and saw a light leaking through a door that was slightly open. He peeked into the room and saw a man on all fours, clawing at the carpet in agony, at the back of the room.

The man was sweating and crying as he prayed to God in a low voice. The friend wondered who it might be, and then realized that it was President Lincoln.

Lincoln was praying earnestly to God: "Please tell me if my ideas are mistaken. Guide me correctly. Please do not make my fellow Americans suffer." Much blood was being shed in the war, and many people were dying on both the North and South sides. It was only natural for the leader of the country to agonize over whether the war was justified or not. This is similar to the question of whether the Vietnam War was just or not. Whether or not a war is a fight for justice is extremely difficult to tell. A leader stands alone and can only pray. He must agonize over whether his decision truly accords with the Will of God or whether it is mistaken because the people under him will all follow his decision. There is no end to this agony.

In Lincoln's case, he suffered a lot every night. He would ask himself, "I oppose slavery, and I don't believe America should be divided into the North and South. I think America must stay united as a country. But does this really accord with God's Will?" That is why, as has been recorded, he was praying at night, digging his nails into the carpet in agony. Just as the pope prays at the Vatican, Lincoln prayed fervently, night after night, like a religious leader. That was Abraham Lincoln. Only a few people may have actually witnessed Lincoln praying, but his virtue seeped out because that was the kind of person he was. It was the leadership of this man that led America to overcome the risk of being divided and to realize an equal society by abolishing slavery.

It is, indeed, tough to be a leader. You cannot solve all problems with your abilities alone; in the end, you need to be in tune with Buddha or God to overcome a national crisis or to lead humanity in the right direction. It is extremely important to have a humble attitude. I hope you will learn from the examples of great historical figures and think about what it means to give love or express unconditional love. There are people in this world who do not care about receiving praise from others or gaining benefits for themselves. These are the people who have illuminated the world throughout the ages.

3
The Correlation Between Virtue and Love

You should not become a leader without knowing the world of the mind

Today, there are various companies all across Japan, so you might think that the country is prospering. However, although capitalist corporations fit into today's society well, they have no heart. This is the biggest flaw. Some people may ask, "Can companies have a heart?" If the word "heart" is unfitting, you could call it "spirit" or a "mindset." In other words, I am talking about a company's purpose.

Each company files articles of incorporation, which contain details of its business, and usually, its business objective is to make a profit. It is fine to chase profit, but what is the profit really for? What is in the minds of the people who seek profit? What exactly is the company's objective? What are the people seeking? Have people ever asked themselves these questions?

I am sure each company teaches its new employees about its business and purpose during orientation. A company has a business objective, and its goal is to make a profit. That is fine. But you must know that profit is essentially neutral in value. Profit itself is neither good nor evil. Whether profit is good or evil is determined by the mindset and motives of the person who uses it and the outcome it brings. Without knowing this, there is no meaning to just increasing the sales figures.

What, then, is important? It is the mindset of the company's leader. From now on, no one should be allowed to stay in a leadership position if they are clueless about the mind. I dare say to those of you who have never disciplined your mind: Leave management immediately. Management is not just about ability. Of course, being competent in itself can be a way to give love to others; it allows you to serve the community. However, if you work for your own gain or to be recognized and rewarded, or if your motive is to benefit yourself, then I must say you have no heart.

What is virtue?

The word *virtue* is often used to describe the qualities needed to become a manager or leader. But virtue has become an outdated word. People nowadays find it hard to understand the importance of virtue. Yet, virtue certainly exists. Let me explain it to you in simple words. A virtuous person is someone who spends the majority of their time in life thinking about other people's happiness.

Now, all of you, look within your minds. What have you thought about in your few decades of life? Has it mainly been about yourself? You can narrow it down to a typical day in your life. Out of the 24 hours, let's say you are awake for 16 hours. What did you think about during those hours? Was it mostly about yourself? Were you only worried about your personal concerns? You may have sometimes thought of others, but were you thinking about their bad points? Were you full of complaints, criticism, or reproaches? Were you always blaming others or your environment? Such people lack virtue.

Virtue is not something that can be taken out and shown to everyone. But ask yourself the following questions: How much time did you spend thinking about love for other people without considering your own benefit or your desire for fame or self-preservation? Did you spend your time wishing to make other people happy? The total amount of time and thoughts you put into doing those things will manifest as virtue.

As your love grows, so will your virtue

In my book, *Rojin, Buddha's Mystical Power*, I explained that the light of enlightenment leaks out from within. Likewise, although the mind is not see-through like glass and is covered by the physical body in this third-dimensional world, light surely seeps out from it. Light leaks out from the mind, as if from inside a silkworm cocoon. This is virtue.

To become a virtuous person, you must be willing to give love to others. Instead of having a give-and-take attitude, it is important to only have a love-that-gives attitude. I have named this kind of love "fundamental love." I have also been teaching that talented people who develop more skills will be able to practice "nurturing love" as they practice giving love. "Nurturing love" is a leader's love; it is a love that teaches and guides others. This stage of love is above the stage of simply giving love. I have said that many leaders of this world practice this type of love. And I have also said that the love that is more difficult to practice than "nurturing love" is the stage of love called "forgiving love."

"Nurturing love" is a love that is practiced by outstanding people. These people can see both the strengths and flaws of others. But at the same time, they develop an acute sense of what is inferior and what is superior, so they start picking on other people's flaws. Most executives struggle with this issue. When people are at the stage of nurturing love, they can see people's flaws too clearly. They pick up on their subordinates' mistakes and weak points too much. Then, like Machiavelli, who wrote *The Prince*, they start to treat people like objects or machines to protect their organization called the "company." They can develop a cold heart in this way.

To overcome this tendency, you need "forgiving love" toward other people. "Forgiving love" is a kind love. It is a feeling of kindness. It is a love that embraces others by forgiving their sins, mistakes, and faults, based on the view that they, too, were created by God and were given life, much like you were. This love arises when your mind has elevated to a religious state.

Then, I stated that above this is "love incarnate," the love of an even greater leader or a great figure. It is the love of someone whose very existence becomes the ethos of the age. Their very presence during a period of time is a gospel to humanity. Such a figure exists at every time and in every region.

The developmental stages of love are the same as the stages in which virtue grows. If I were to point out a difference, I would say that love manifests in actions. Love manifests in people's activities. Love is born between people. Love appears in relationships between people. Thoughts take form and manifest in a visible way through deeds or activities, and we call this action "love." On the other hand, virtue has an emphasis on existence itself, rather than action or activity. Virtue can also be explained as the profound wisdom that is stored in your mind. When love sublimates and crystallizes into a gem, it becomes virtue.

Words for Leaders 1
The Winning Strategy

Is there a way you can always win
Regardless of the situation?
Many have sought the answer to this question
Since time immemorial.
Indeed, there is a winning strategy.
It certainly exists in each of your minds.
First, be wise.
Next, be loving.
Then, be courageous.

Wisdom, love, and courage—
These elements give rise to virtue,
And they also make up a winning strategy.
Refine your wisdom,
Enrich your capacity for love,
And summon up more courage.
Then, a path will surely open for you.

Part II

A Leader's Blind Spot

–Constantly Work on Your Foundations

CHAPTER SIX

Building the Foundations and Focusing on Your Strengths

1
Continue Building Stronger Foundations

A distinctive trait among people who make profound decisions and take responsible actions

Let us consider the foundations for life. After all, whether or not firm foundations have been established is vital to everything. This is as true for an individual as it is for a large corporation; without a firm base, an individual or company will be weak. The same can be said about any type of work. In every aspect of life, strong foundations are important.

For example, I believe that the main purpose of school education is to lay strong foundations for life. Those who have negative views of education systems often criticize school education as a waste of time, saying that individuals should be free to study whatever they like and as much as they like. However, it cannot be denied that a well-rounded education is beneficial in creating a firm foundation for life.

Throughout our lives, we make decisions and take action on many different issues. In order to do that, we need information, motivation, and basic skills to base our decisions and actions on. People cannot make decisions or take action without having accumulated these things.

Thus, it is very important to have firm foundations in life. The more solid and dense your foundations are, the more profound and responsible your decisions and actions will be.

Are you continuing to build stronger foundations for your life?

Sometimes, look at yourself and ask if you are making daily efforts to build the foundations on which you base your life. If your foundations are inadequate, you will find that things do not go smoothly in many situations. Building your foundations should not be limited to childhood. Even as an adult, you should continue to build your foundations steadily and persistently.

People tend to place importance on producing, but if they focus only on producing without absorbing, they will become exhausted before long. The same can be said for professions. For instance, there will be a great difference between pharmacists who continue to acquire and absorb new information about medicine and those who have not acquired new knowledge since graduating from university. This is also true of company employees. There is a world of difference between those who simply do the work they are given and those who constantly study, acquiring new information about the economy or other knowledge that helps them do a better job. This difference is especially apparent among engineers. Those who are always experimenting day after day, seeking to improve their skills, will eventually succeed in developing new technologies.

So, instead of being satisfied with establishing your foundations once and then neglecting them, strive day by day to build the foundations of your life. Even if you do not get immediate results, it is all the more important that you build foundations that will give you good results in three, five, or even ten years.

2

How Strong Is Your Determination to Study?

Ask yourself if you are satisfied with the way you are now

When I had just started working at a trading company, I would get up at 5:45 a.m. every morning before sunrise and read 10 pages of *Self-Help* by Samuel Smiles. Please excuse me for bringing this up, but I did it in my dormitory restroom. While it was still dark outside, I read under the white fluorescent light, thinking, "I want to be someone who can make a difference in the world." As I read and learned that the British Empire prospered because many people with the spirit of self-help worked very hard, I thought that I, too, could become a person like that if I made diligent efforts. I worked toward this ideal, and it became a reality after about 10 years.

The key is to ask yourself whether you are satisfied with who you are now and to pull yourself up by your bootstraps if you are not. Most people do not necessarily possess any one particular outstanding talent. If this is true for you, one of the keys to success in life is to invest as much time as you can into what is most important for you without wasting a single moment—including your time in the early morning. This will bring you the highest chance of success.

Give up on things you consider a waste of time. You may have all kinds of obligations and things you feel like you have to do, but you need to realize early on that your limited talents will never make you distinguished if you live ordinarily like everyone else. Those who realize this early have an advantage. People usually start regretting things around the time they retire, so it is important to realize this early in life. When you know that your talents are not particularly outstanding, but you nevertheless want to accomplish meaningful work, you must stop wasting your time and instead invest all of your time in what is most important to you.

Keep your battles to your main work

Some office workers feel obliged to socialize with their colleagues after work and end up having a drink almost every night. As they become unable to break this habit, they become like hungry ghosts in hell and try to drag others in as well. They may coerce other colleagues into staying and socializing. Many may even say something like, "You know I won't let you go, right?" If you are bound by "shackles" like this and cannot free yourself from them, I must say that you are the one who is responsible for your situation.

People in this kind of situation probably believe they need to fulfill social obligations to be promoted. However, people who believe this are likely to be incredibly incompetent at work; they work hard in their "side work" because they lack self-confidence in their main work. But the real battle lies within the eight-hour workday, so they must go back to basics and fight the battle in their main work. If they are a useful and beneficial employee to the company, they will not be treated poorly. As long as they do their work well, it will not be easy to transfer or demote them simply because they refuse to go out for drinks. If they do get transferred or demoted nevertheless, it probably means their company is heading for bankruptcy. In that case, it would be a good idea to "spin off" from them and leave early. So, please do not blame others; instead, hold yourself accountable.

Think about how to make more time

It is also important to make the most of the weekend. The basic rule is this: Use one day for socializing, exercising, or other activities, and the other day for resting and recovering.

I write many books and give many lectures. What made all of it possible? I considered how much time I had spent reading and studying before I was able to do what I do now and found that I had spent tens of thousands of hours. Not just thousands of hours—I created tens of thousands of hours. I somehow managed to squeeze all of that time in.

Each day only has 24 hours, so you need to find a way to make time. It is your own responsibility to do so. People who do not make their own time are too easy on themselves and are simply making excuses by saying, "I don't have time." You must find time no matter what. For example, you can read quite a lot just on your daily commute during the week. If the commute is two hours by public transportation, a fast reader could finish a whole book in a day's commute. Even a slow reader could finish one over the course of five days. Further, if you set aside time for reading on either Saturday or Sunday, you can read a considerable number of pages.

When I used to work at a trading company, I had very little time for myself, so I would shut myself in for at least one day of the weekend; I decided not to let anyone disturb me. I would participate in social obligations for work on one of the days of the weekend if I had no other choice, but I absolutely would not allow anyone to bother me on the other day. No matter how much my colleagues bad-mouthed me, I stuck to this principle. When I could not read as much as I wanted during the week, I would tear through about six books on Saturday, even at the risk of ruining my eyesight. Nowadays, I can read about 20 books a day, but back then, my eyes would hurt after reading about six books a day. Even so, I was fully determined to read all the books I had planned to read that week. Every time I went to a bookstore, I would buy 20 to 30 books and stack them up on my desk. I had it set up so that the only way to clear my desk was to read them all, one by one. When I was too busy to read books for several days, I had no other choice but to find time and read them all at once. I was determined to keep reading and studying even if I had to drag myself to do it. These efforts have made me who I am today. There is not that big a difference in people's abilities, so you will end up becoming just like everyone else unless you push yourself hard.

3

Developing Your Strengths Based on the 80-20 Rule

How you allocate your time is the key to success

You must be aware that you only have 24 hours in a day and your abilities are limited. Therefore, if you are going to live this restricted kind of life for decades, you should concentrate on what truly resonates with your soul and accords with your inner ideals. If you think you have unlimited talent, then this is not a problem for you. But if you do not feel this way, it is essential to allocate your limited supply of time to what you believe to be most important or meaningful. This is the key to a successful life.

As I mentioned in the previous section, I used to work for a trading company, so I had a lot of opportunities to socialize. What I can say is that it is very important not to become too absorbed in certain things. I would put 80 percent of my energy into my main work and the remaining 20 percent into others. With the 20 percent, I expanded my experience but did not get too deeply involved in activities I was not very good at. This was my policy. The important key here is to secure the core of your work. Once you secure the core, you will be on your way to boundless success.

You will gradually gain the power of influence as you work to refine and develop yourself

People can make continual efforts toward something they find most valuable. They can tirelessly devote five, ten, or twenty years to it. On the other hand, if they feel something is meaningless, they cannot do it for so long. Therefore, if you are aware that you have limited abilities, you must not turn away from the effort needed to bring out your best in order for you to succeed. Since there are only 24 hours in a day, it is sensible to consider how to use them to live the best life possible. This is one of the modern practical applications of the Middle Way, taught in Buddhism.

As you refine yourself, you should become a good influence on others. There are times in life when you are wasting time, but if that is the case, it is important to select and value the experiences that will serve to polish your soul. It is foolish to spend 100 percent of your time on things you are not really interested in. But you should not spend 100 percent of your time on yourself because you will lose the opportunity to be an inspiration to others. It is therefore important to develop yourself first and gradually exert your influence on others.

CHAPTER SEVEN

Always Observe and Prepare for What Is Ahead

1
How to Acquire Depth and Strength as a Leader

Looking at those who become leaders and guide others, it is obvious that their knowledge is not limited to what they learned at school; rather, they have wisdom that comes from discoveries they have made through numerous experiences. It is this wisdom that gives them the depth and strength of character to lead others.

You may have had the chance to listen to talks given by Happy Science lecturers. Whatever you may feel inspired by in their talks comes from the valuable discoveries they have made throughout their lives. A talk given by someone who has accumulated wisdom through discoveries is often very insightful. On the other hand, the speech of someone who has not discovered much will sound somewhat bland and shallow. The difference lies in whether the speaker has been living aimlessly or has been making many meaningful discoveries in their life.

Experience does not mean simply growing older; it is the sum total of everything a person has discovered and grasped over the course of their life. I would especially like to point out to young people that careful observation is most important in making discoveries. When you are still young, your brain is sharp, so it is easier to absorb knowledge. But you can only improve the quality of your discoveries through keen observation.

Therefore, observe many people carefully, for they are a source of learning material. Study the way they think and act. Ask yourself how a successful person would act in a particular situation, and also watch how those who fail behave when faced with a similar situation. As you continue observing others, you will build up a body of knowledge without necessarily having to undergo the same experiences yourself. By watching others, you can learn things that lie outside your own personal experience. This is very important to remember.

2

How to Avoid the Peter Principle at Work

People who become incompetent after a promotion

The seniority system can often cause a company to go out of business. Under this system, you may appoint someone as an executive solely because he has reached a certain age, for example. Or you may promote a person to a higher position out of pity because they had "big hits" a long time ago. This kind of practice can be observed not only in Japan but also in other countries.

There are people who become incompetent as soon as they advance to a higher position, even if they had been competent up to that point. This is called the Peter Principle. For example, highly competent rank-and-file employees may suddenly become incompetent after being promoted to a senior staff position. This happens because their abilities fall short of the requirements for senior staff. There are also those who were highly competent as senior staff but start to perform poorly once they become section chiefs due to their inability to manage others. As senior staff, they may have worked hard to serve their superiors, but as section chiefs, they are unable to lead others due to a lack of management skills.

There are others who used to excel as section chiefs but suddenly become inept once they become department heads. Although they could handle the line management duties as section chiefs, they must now manage other managers as department heads. But because they lack the skills and knowledge to teach and instruct other managers, they tend to stick to the work of section chiefs even after becoming department heads. When a department head does the work of section chiefs, it deprives the section chiefs of their work and forces them to do work that people in a lower position are doing. As a result, an incompetent department head will end up wasting other people's time rather than creating it.

Further, there are those who were highly competent as department heads but become useless once they become executives. These people can effectively manage line managers, but as soon as they are put in a position to oversee the entire company with a holistic perspective, they suddenly get sidelined. Although they go to the office every morning, they have nothing to do but read the newspaper; they have no documents on their desks and no real work to do. Someone in this position is in a difficult situation. People who leave after about two years of being promoted to an executive position usually fit this description.

Make preparations ahead of time to eliminate your worries

The "Peter Principle" exists and unfortunately applies to a good percentage of people. It is indeed true that some people, who may be performing well in their current position, become incompetent once they are promoted to a higher position. This happens due to the change in the type of work they need to do. Unless you train yourself and improve your skills so you can handle higher-level work and manage many people, your promotion can be detrimental and cause you to suffer. Although you may have worked with vigor and purpose as a section chief, you might begin to perform poorly the moment you become a department head. So, a promotion can either be good or bad. It is hard to tell whether the promotion will lead to celebration or become a path to resignation.

Then, what do you need to do to avoid being trapped by the Peter Principle? For example, before becoming a section chief, put yourself in the shoes of a section chief and think about what it would be like to do the work. If you feel ready to become a section chief, you will not fall behind when you actually become one. In the same way, if you start preparing yourself to become a department head while you are still a section chief and do so years in advance, you will perform well when you actually become one.

The important thing is to always make preparations ahead of time. Always ask yourself whether you will be able to do your superior's work when you get promoted in a few years, and keep observing and studying your superior's work so that you know what to do when you assume that position. You can never be too prepared. Always observe and learn the elements, mindset, and abilities required to do higher-level work. Those who are likely to become CEOs in the future not only do their own work but also pay close attention to their company's overall activities and philosophy, even when they are still new hires. They observe and contemplate what is on their CEO's mind. Unfortunately, those who show no interest in anything other than their own work will not be able to advance to higher positions in the company.

3

Vividly Visualize Your Future Work and Position

People attract a future that best suits their caliber

According to organizational psychology, a group of eight people is the optimal or maximum size for a section to function well. Let us say there is a competent section chief who bases his self-image on this standard. Someone like him may gradually lose control of his subordinates when the number of people in his section exceeds ten. He may lose track of what his subordinates are doing or thinking, and may even forget their names. Such a person can only visualize himself managing up to eight people.

On the other hand, there are also people in society who aspire to manage about 50 subordinates, even if they are currently just supervising eight people. They believe that they are capable of doing this and visualize it in their minds. Those who can imagine their ideal selves clearly in this way will eventually be promoted to actually work with 50 subordinates.

This does not happen to those who are unable to visualize themselves in this way. They will fail somewhere along the way or blow their chances of getting promoted, and settle into a position that best suits their caliber. They may make a slip of the tongue or say something inappropriate just as they are about to get promoted, and ruin their chances completely.

The cause of unexpected failures

Suppose someone has been recognized as extremely capable and is on track to become a department head soon. During a meeting, he may expose the fact that he lacks common knowledge and does not know the basic terminology that any executive would. In reality, there are many things people do not know, no matter who they are. But having their lack of knowledge exposed in a public setting means that they lack good luck as well. This usually happens to those who are unable to visualize themselves holding a higher position. People usually end up settling in the position that is most appropriate for them.

This is how things are. Thinking about how many people you will be able to manage when you become a leader will generally reveal the position that you will end up in in the future.

4

Living Strategically Makes Your Worries Seem Trivial

You can be extraordinary even with ordinary abilities

It is very important to live strategically. A person with a certain level of wisdom and ability will use various tactics to solve problems that arise daily, weekly, or monthly. However, very few people live strategically.

There are considerably fewer people who look at least three years ahead when deciding on their current lifestyle or activities. Those who are capable of doing this are already out of the ordinary. Even if their abilities may be ordinary, their thinking is extraordinary, which will make them seem like extraordinary people in the end. People like this have already considered ideas that others in the same industry or those who started out around the same time as they did have not yet considered, and are advancing steadily toward realizing them. The very fact that they have established this style of living already makes them extraordinary.

As long as you have created a vessel, it does not matter whether it is filled or not; others cannot tell the difference so easily. If you make a one-liter bottle, for example, you can fill it up with one liter's worth of liquid. If your bottle is small and can only hold one-tenth of a liter, you will never be able to fill it more than that. But with a one-liter bottle, you will be able to put more than what a one-tenth-of-a-liter bottle could hold, if you want to. Even if you do not fill the bottle yourself, the rain could fall and fill it for you. So, it does not matter whether the vessel is filled at the moment. The important thing is to build a vessel first. To build a big vessel, it is essential to live your life strategically.

Do not let trivial worries bring you down

To live strategically, first set your ideal or goal. Then, work backward and think about what you need to do at each stage to get there. Look three, ten, or twenty years ahead, and work backward. If you can figure out where you should be in ten years, you can then think about what you must accomplish in five years and then three years to achieve that goal. Thinking in this way will allow you to clearly see what path you should be taking right now. This strategic approach can also be applied to your everyday life. In other words, living life strategically will prevent you from being caught up in trivial worries.

You may think about various things and worry that you will be crushed by the weight of an extremely difficult problem, but in reality, the little things are what cause you to fail. Things that are meant to happen will happen; accidents may occur, too. You may not be able to avoid all the difficulties that befall you. Perhaps, many unpleasant things will happen one after another within a single day. However, you must not let yourself be defeated by insignificant problems at that time. Do not amplify small problems into a major life problem. Instead, live strategically. You should always think about the kind of person you want to be in 10 years or 50 years. As long as you have this aspiration, things will not seem like such a big deal, even if you are scolded by your superior and have to apologize.

As a basic strategy, think of yourself as someone who does not belong where you currently are. Tell yourself, "I just happen to be in this illusory situation for a short time. This is their world, and it has nothing to do with me," and decisively stop worrying about trifling matters. Then, you will be able to develop a mindset that is considerably stronger and detach yourself from things that are not a big deal. Cast aside everyday trifles by living strategically, and think about things on a larger scale.

CHAPTER EIGHT

Building Up the Caliber to Withstand Adversities

1

Do Not Lead a Life of Excuses

Make sure to learn lessons, especially in times of adversity

During times of misfortune, try not to feel that you are the only person who is suffering. Others are also suffering from illness, setbacks, or failures. People tend to feel that they are the only ones who are facing misfortune.

When adversity strikes, open your eyes, open your heart, and observe many other people. You will realize that people who are blessed with good fortune are not the only ones who succeed. Among the successful are certainly people who have faced failure or adversity but have made the utmost effort to succeed by using their misfortune as a springboard.

There was a U.S. president who was confined to a wheelchair. Being confined to a wheelchair usually makes it difficult to take part in social activities, but he fulfilled his duties as president. Unlike ordinary people who would quickly depend on others, he did what he could and did not lead a life of excuses. He made every effort to overcome his disability. He was an exemplary person in this way.

People like him have certainly been able to grasp important life lessons in the midst of adversity. There are common traits among those who, despite adversity, achieve heights that ordinary people could never reach.

Four common traits of successful people

Here are the common traits of successful people: First, they never attribute their adversities or hardships to others. They never blame others or bemoan their fate, because they know very well that doing so will not do any good.

The second trait is that they accept what fate has given them. They do not complain by saying, "If only it had never happened." Instead, they accept whatever adversity has come their way. By doing this, they see it as reality and consider how to overcome it. They have the determination and courage to accept reality and any misfortunes they experience.

The third trait is that they always find a lesson in adversity. They ask themselves what the difficulty they are facing is trying to teach them, and always find the answer. These lessons remain in their hearts as treasures for years to come.

The fourth trait is that they are independent and never rely on other people's support. Even if they find themselves in disadvantageous circumstances, they stand on their own two feet and walk their path with an indomitable and independent spirit. To put it simply, they never forget the spirit of self-help. They see their fate as something given to them and accept their present state for what it is. Yet, they are not complacent with the status quo. Instead, they strive to break free of their difficulties with their own strength. All successful people have gone through this process.

People who tend to wallow in self-pity will never achieve great success. There are probably many people who are tempted to do so, but once they start seeking sympathy from others, they will continually try to get pity from others throughout their lives. There are people who had been enjoying the golden years of their career until just recently who may bemoan their misfortune, while others may complain about a physical disability or illness they have contracted. However, deciding to depend on others for help after facing difficulties like these means defeat for their souls. They must accept their fate bravely and be determined to overcome it.

2

People Without Patience End Up Digging Their Own Grave

Persevere for another six months

One of the things that cause evil to arise is bad timing. A good action can become evil if you choose the wrong timing or opportunity. Let me explain this using company management as an example. Even a promising company can fail if it starts expanding its business a year ahead of schedule without considering its capacity based on its current staffing and financial situation. This is a natural consequence. There are countless cases in which companies without sufficient capital decide to advertise heavily with hopes of attracting customers, only to fail and suffer financial difficulties. A business can succeed if it still has room for growth and strategically decides to expand after building a proven track record. But if they take a desperate gamble, like the Japanese Kamikaze Special Attack Unit during World War II, and invest all the company's capital to expand the business, they will ultimately end in failure. This happens all too often. It is a good example of what happens when you fail to choose the right timing.

When I observe the pattern of people who fail, many seem to have trouble with the issue of timing. One of the most common reasons people fail in life is impatience. There are a surprising number of cases in which people end up digging their own graves simply because they cannot wait six months for the situation to turn around, and instead, run around in confusion, making unnecessary choices on their own.

If you listen to your heart carefully and reflect on whether you have acted this way, perhaps 70 to 80 percent of you will realize that you have. Those of you who envision yourselves failing or have the mindset of failure will struggle alone and end up digging your own grave, even when things would otherwise go smoothly if you do not miss the right timing or opportunity.

Unnecessary moves keep you even further from success

It is not rare for people to make a blunder just when they are about to achieve success. This can happen right before a promotion, too.

Let us say there is an employee named Mr. A. He is on the promotion list and his superiors are planning to promote him to section chief in the next personnel transfer in April. But suppose Mr. A is feeling distressed by the delay in his promotion because Mr. B, who joined the company at the same time as him, was already promoted to section chief in October of last year. Mr. A's superiors are evaluating him fairly and believe he deserves to become section chief in April because his performance is on par with Mr. B's. However, being unable to wait these six months, Mr. A may start to speak ill of his colleague who was promoted early. He may say, "It's not fair. My performance is no different from Mr. B's and may actually be better than his. How come he could become section chief before me? He must have curried favor with his superiors quite extensively or even resorted to an underhanded approach." These remarks of Mr. A may eventually reach his superiors' ears and make them think, "Although we wanted to promote both Mr. A and Mr. B to section chiefs back then, there was only one position available at the time. That's why we tried hard to open up another position by April. But look how Mr. A is talking badly about Mr. B. Perhaps we should reconsider appointing someone like him to the position of section chief. Maybe we should wait another six months to make sure our decision isn't mistaken." This may cause Mr. A's promotion to be delayed once again. Meanwhile, Mr. A may continue to come up with various schemes to get ahead, only to put himself in an even more disadvantageous position. In the end, he may start to blame the company's ineptitude at allocating personnel until he completely ruins his chances of becoming a section chief. An extremely large number of people end up like this. There are many people who are very likely to end up the same way. These people need to develop the awareness to know when the timing is right.

You need to be aware that ignorance can sometimes become a sin. The fact that you do not know is not anyone else's responsibility but your own. That is why you need to make efforts to raise your level of awareness. If you can remain composed and focused on your work even when your colleague is promoted ahead of you, your superior will notice the greatness of your character and feel regretful for not having given you the treatment you deserve. Then, your promotion may come earlier than expected. But if you are unaware of your superior's considerations and resort to unnecessary moves to be promoted, your promotion will be delayed even further. Unfortunately, those who are in this situation are unable to see what is going on.

Opportunities will come your way if you keep refining yourself

It is often said that perseverance pays off. A path will eventually open for those who continue to develop their abilities and accumulate inner strength, as if collecting water in a jar one drop at a time. These people usually have the ability to carve out a path on their own, but others will definitely come to help them as well. Those who are emitting light rarely go unnoticed by others in society.

You may complain that others do not acknowledge your effort or that they do not give you the treatment you deserve, but there are countless people in the world who are looking to help you open a path at any chance they get. Even so, many people fail to notice the "fishing line" that has been dropped in front of them and run around aimlessly, only to ruin their chances completely. When you feel that you have not been given proper acknowledgment, you should work on letting your inner diamond shine. To put it another way, when the spotlight does not shine on you, tell yourself that your time has yet to come and focus on developing your abilities further. This is the secret to a successful life. Someone who has continued to hone their abilities for five to ten years will eventually be spotted by others, without fail. But in reality, many people do not have the capacity to persevere long enough, which means they have no hope of success anyway. Please keep this in mind.

3

Know Your Capacity and Restrain Your Desires

You will have the outcome most appropriate for you

Nowadays, new shops and restaurants open successively in the food service industry, but according to a survey from several years ago, roughly 75 percent of newly opened shops and restaurants in Japan close down within three years. The owners of chain stores probably aspire to expand their businesses to hundreds or thousands of locations nationwide, but in reality, their businesses are not the only ones that exist. There are plenty of other franchises that offer similar services and products; similar coffee shops, noodle shops, and supermarkets exist everywhere. The fact that 75 percent of shops and restaurants close within three years of opening means that excessive competition is driving some businesses to go under within the same industry. Because the population of Japan is hardly growing now, the excess number of businesses ultimately leads to weaker businesses being weeded out according to customer needs.

This reality may be hard to accept for business owners who only think of their own company's growth. However, they need to shift their viewpoint and look at their businesses from a bigger perspective. They need to examine carefully what kinds of efforts their competitors are making and what products or services their customers are choosing. From this perspective, they need to be able to determine the appropriate size and capacity of their business and the level of fame they deserve.

So, you need to know that the most appropriate outcome will come to you. While your hopes certainly will come true, you must also know that the higher your ideals are, the more difficult it will be to achieve them.

Restrain your desires and prepare yourself for the next opportunity

We all have desires, and to a certain degree, they serve as the driving force for our growth. Having said that, as our desires expand, we sometimes trip over our own feet because of these desires and find that things do not go as we had hoped. Just as many oyster shells accumulate at the bottom of a boat, we accumulate various desires in the process of our development, which sometimes hinder us from growing further. Other people's ideas and how we interact with others may also bind us and stop us from making progress straightforwardly. While we can work happily by following our desires and expanding them, once we have achieved a certain level of growth, we must next learn to abandon and restrain our desires. The principle of success can vary depending on our level of growth in this way.

In spear fighting, it is said that withdrawing the spear is more difficult than thrusting it forward and that becoming a master spearman requires the skill to pull the spear back at a considerable speed. This is because the spear is inactive when it remains thrust into the enemy. People who can pull the spear back quickly can use it more freely for longer and reach farther. Likewise, it is sometimes important to "withdraw" your desires. Desires tend to grow more and more, but if you think certain desires are not appropriate to your current caliber and ability, or you find that it is not the right time to act on those desires, you should restrain them and prepare for the next opportunity. Those who can do this will be able to enjoy continued success.

CHAPTER NINE

Produce Positive Results by Using Your Personnel Effectively

1
Listen to Opinions That Are Different from Yours

The characteristics of competent people with leadership qualities

Capable people are generally talkative until about 30 years of age. They are often quick-witted, so they talk a lot and reach their own conclusions even before their superiors have finished explaining things to them. The moment their superiors start explaining a task, they respond with, "OK, I got it," and begin working on it immediately without listening to the explanation until the end.

However, from around age 30, some of them gradually become less talkative and start to listen to the opinions of others. Even if someone gives an opinion that sounds foolish, they will still listen and think, "Perhaps that's another way to see this" or "Maybe there's some truth in what he says." They will no longer just adhere to their own views, but will also consider other people's opinions and see if there are any useful ideas in them. Even if they do not take in someone else's views, they still evaluate them positively for having different or opposing opinions.

This compares to when they were younger, where they would quickly debate people who expressed different opinions and rejoice in victory, whereas at this age, they gradually begin to display a different approach that comes from experience.

Your caliber as a leader makes you more convincing

There is a big difference between pushing things forward without knowing what the opposing opinions are and charging ahead with your own way while being fully aware of them. Although they may look the same, they are in fact completely different.

If you move forward with an understanding of the different views that people hold, you will start to display a special quality or depth in the way you work. Even though it may look the same on the outside, people around you will somehow sense the difference and become more convinced of your intention. They will sense the "leaking light" and will tell themselves, "This person is aware of other people's views and knows that other approaches can work as well. Even so, he is taking this approach, so there must be a deeper level of thought behind his decision." On the other hand, people will remain indifferent toward those who only focus on winning over others and will stand ready to ridicule them should they ever fail.

People will approve of and follow leaders who understand opposing views well, even when they adopt a different approach. They can sense that their leaders will change their minds and adopt an opposing view if they find that a decision they made proved wrong. In contrast, leaders who see others as rivals and immediately crush opposing views will never accept an idea that contradicts their own. This difference in attitude shows one's capacity as a leader. Whether or not you can develop this capacity will determine whether you can grow into a great leader.

2
The Three Conditions That a Manager Must Satisfy

The qualities of a competent leader

Let me now discuss the leadership qualities required of company managers. Being a leader in a company means holding a higher position than others, which applies to anyone from senior staff to section chief, general manager, director, executive director, and all the way up to CEO. So that I can discuss leadership, I will refer to all of these positions as "management" and consider what people in management positions should be like.

To be in a management position, at least the following three conditions must be met. First, leaders must be capable of making higher-level decisions. They should have excellent decision-making ability and be able to reach the right conclusions. Second, leaders need to serve as educators who can train and guide their subordinates. Third, leaders need to be aware that they are in a position to determine whether their subordinates become financially happy or unhappy. To be more specific, they have the power to decide whether to raise or cut their employees' salaries and bonuses, thereby determining their sense of happiness. These three abilities—decision-making, training and education, and determining proper financial compensation for their employees—are required of those in management positions. They also serve as criteria for measuring leadership capability.

1) Competence accompanied by virtue

The first condition—being capable of making difficult, higher-level decisions—requires leaders to be competent. In other words, they need to be experts in their job. I am not going to delve into this topic in this book because I am sure most people are aware that it is an essential ability that they need to cultivate as a leader, and many companies probably offer training to help their employees develop this skill. But there is one thing I want to emphasize: Leaders are required to have foresight. They need to be able to foresee what is to come.

While it is possible to serve as a competent manager for a certain period, whether someone can remain competent for years to come is another issue. For example, people can produce good results within a six-month to one-year timeframe, but some are only interested in doing well in their current position and may not contribute to the company's long-term growth. Their main concern is to achieve good results that will benefit them during their tenure of, say, two years, and they do not care about what happens to the company after they leave. In reality, since employees are assessed based on their performance in their current role, they cannot receive a salary raise or a promotion unless they achieve solid results in that role. So we can, of course, argue that there is something wrong with this assessment system. It sometimes results in many problems being found when managers are replaced.

Some managers have the discretion to make deals, but do so even at the cost of hurting the company after their tenure. They may promise their clients future returns to gain immediate profits, or do whatever it takes to make a profitable deal for the first few years, but in doing so, leave their successors all kinds of problems to take care of. These managers cause trouble for the company and those who replace them in later years. Therefore, when it comes to the ultimate decision-making ability or the ability to get work done, I hope all managers will strive to accumulate virtue in areas that do not directly affect their personal performance. While they can allocate 60 to 70 percent of their time and energy to tasks that directly contribute to their personal performance, they should use the remaining 30 to 40 percent to lay the groundwork for those who will come after them and to contribute to their company's future development. Managers should always keep these two goals in mind as they engage in their day-to-day work.

2) Accumulating specialized knowledge and understanding the human mind

The second condition of leadership is the quality of being an educator, which is often undervalued. In general, people are evaluated by their competence at work, but their ability to train and educate others is, unfortunately, not valued as highly. In fact, competent people often preoccupy themselves with doing well in their own work, even at the expense of others, while educators who can nurture and guide others often fall behind in the rat race and end up being assigned unimportant tasks. However, since companies should be training grounds for building character in the coming age, they need to highlight and value educational skills in managers.

So, what conditions must managers meet to serve as educators? As a starting point, they need expertise, or accumulated specialized knowledge, so that they can teach the people who work under them. Another condition is that they have a good understanding of human beings. We cannot teach others or bring out the best in them unless we get to know them deeply. Therefore, leaders need to accumulate specialized knowledge and have a deep understanding of the human mind. If you aspire to work your way up to a management position, you need to develop a breadth of knowledge about human beings and broaden the scope of your life experience in advance. This ability to teach and guide others will be in demand and valued even more in the coming age.

3) Straighten yourself and make fair judgments

Third, those in management positions need to understand that they hold important keys that determine whether their subordinates end up rich or poor, because they will be evaluating their job performance. It is the managers' job to decide whether their subordinates deserve a raise, a promotion, or an increase in their bonus. So, it is no exaggeration to say that their subordinates' economic well-being depends on the decisions that they make.

Managers must first realize that they can make their subordinates either happy or unhappy in an economic sense. That is why they must always strive to evaluate them fairly. They must straighten themselves, treat people equally, and make fair judgments as though they are judging on behalf of God. They should never favor specific people or evaluate people based on their personal likes and dislikes.

Impartiality cannot be cultivated through school education or social training alone. These efforts are not enough. To foster a spirit of fairness, you need to make your mind upright, and to do this, you must seek a higher level of spirituality. Straighten yourself, be humble, and devote yourself to a Greater Being. Since you are in a position to influence other people's happiness or unhappiness, you need to evaluate them as though you are performing sacred work. This last point—non-subjective judgment—is extremely important for managers.

3
Discerning Other People's Destiny

The appointment of Admiral Togo led Japan to victory in the Japanese-Russian War

In war, appointing the right person to a crucial leadership position, such as the Commander-in-Chief of the Combined Fleet, can lead a nation to decisive victory, whereas appointing the wrong person can result in defeat and possibly even 50 to 100 years of hardship for its people.

When we examine how the Japanese Imperial Military selected its leaders in World War II—its Admirals, Vice Admirals, and Rear Admirals—we can find many mistakes. They appointed men to leadership positions to fight the war based on a bureaucratic promotion system, so unfortunately, they failed to appoint the right men to the right positions.

In contrast, during the Japanese-Russian War, they commissioned Heihachiro Togo, who, until then, had not been the star of the class, as Commander-in-Chief of the Combined Fleet, bypassing other high-ranking men above him. Togo was recognized for having luck on his side, demonstrating virtuous character, and faithfully carrying out the orders he received from headquarters.

These were the reasons he was singled out for promotion to this position over other men. Until then, he had been considered too small in frame for a command post and had demonstrated little sign of military brilliance. So, by the time he was appointed captain, everyone had expected him to be heading toward retirement.

But, as history has shown, he was a man fit to be a leader. The decision to appoint him Commander-in-Chief ultimately led Japan to victory in the Japanese-Russian War. Had it been someone else, Japan might well have suffered a devastating defeat against the Russians, which could have led to a completely different aftermath.

Choose a person who is guided by heaven

To be successful, it is often not enough to rely on your abilities alone. A vital element of success is found in choosing the right people to support you. You need to develop an exceptional eye for people. This means that you need to cultivate the ability to recognize people's talents and abilities, as well as whether they are naturally blessed with good fortune. Credentials and personal history may indicate what the individual accomplished in the past, but you will not be able to determine other aspects such as the unique aura they emanate. In other words, you also need to discern whether they are the type of person who receives the support of their guardian and guiding spirits in heaven.

Those with divine assistance can accomplish more than they can alone because they receive all kinds of help from the Spirit World. Placing people like this into positions of leadership will attract many others who want to offer their support. On the other hand, when people under the influence of evil spirits, instead of divine spirits, are appointed to leadership positions, they will attract people who act like the minions of evil spirits. So, it is important to be able to tell what type of person other people truly are. Having people on your side who share your aspirations will be a tremendous source of strength.

Words for Leaders 2

The Royal Road to Success

The way to success is not very difficult.
I want to tell you that
There is a very simple method.
However, what makes this simple method difficult
Is the fact that you must commit to it continuously.
You may feel motivated for a while,
But it is hard to keep making efforts.
First, be cheerful.
First, be positive.
First, be healthy.
First, be diligent.

First, have a heart of gratitude toward all people,
And always walk the path of effort.
All the keys to success lie hidden in these attitudes.
The rest is persistence and consistency.
Whether you can do this or not
Will determine whether you become a success or a failure.

Part III

An Innovator Who Keeps Creating Value

CHAPTER TEN

Fight According to the Size of Your Organization and Your Circumstances

1
The Strategy for the Weak and the Strategy for the Strong

The necessary perspectives to analyze your organization with

It is extremely rare for one particular organization to be the best in all aspects. Every organization has both strengths and weaknesses. Therefore, you need to identify your organization's strengths and strive to win in those areas, while skillfully making up for its weaknesses to minimize damage to your organization. Knowing your organization's strengths and weaknesses is one perspective to consider when you are analyzing it.

Another perspective to analyze your organization with is to figure out where it stands within the industry. A small-scale organization will be considered "weak," while a large-scale organization will be considered "strong." So, depending on where your organization sits, the strategies to adopt will naturally differ. Deciding on appropriate strategies is a subtle matter, and here lies the difficulty of management.

People in management positions must first assess the scale of their organization, identify whether it is weak or strong, and then develop their strategy accordingly. They must also consider the strengths and weaknesses within their organization. For example, a company may have ample capital and be strong in terms of capital accumulation but be weak in terms of technology. Another company may lack capital but instead have advanced technologies. There may be other companies that lack both capital and technology but have superior public relations skills. Each organization has unique characteristics, strengths, and weaknesses, so it is essential to develop strategies and tactics that suit them.

The strategy for the weak

As a general rule, the weak cannot defeat the strong in an all-out battle. This is a basic principle. So, if you think your organization is categorized as weak, you must fight and win your battles using the strengths it has.

Despite their size, some small companies are extremely advanced when it comes to technology. They have specific technology that is so advanced that even large companies cannot compete in this particular area. Companies like this should focus on that specific area and make an all-out effort to win in that space. This strategy is what is commonly known as "focusing on a niche." A niche refers to a specialized market that large companies avoid focusing on. When you focus all your efforts on competing in a particular niche, you will be able to open a new path for your company. However, if the niche market grows beyond a certain size, large companies with substantial capital may enter and take it over. If this happens, you need to think about your next move. You can either grow your company further to compete with them or look for another niche.

The basic strategy for the weak lies in targeting a niche market or a small market that has been left untouched. The weak must target markets that the strong have overlooked or not targeted, and use unexpected approaches to compete in the market. A small company cannot win against an industry giant in an all-out battle. But even an industry giant has weaknesses, and small companies may have particular strengths. By focusing on those strengths, small companies can win. Large companies are usually spread out too widely from having expanded their business, so to win against them, small companies should compete in areas where large companies have let their guard down. This is the strategy for the weak.

The strategy for the strong

The strategy for the strong is the opposite: focus on surrounding small opponents with a larger force. The Japanese feudal lord Hideyoshi Toyotomi (1537 - 1598) was good at executing this strategy and often employed it, especially after he unified the country. He would carefully compare his forces to the enemy's, and when the enemy had a larger army—even just by one soldier—he would avoid battle, choose reconciliation, and rely on his diplomatic skills to negotiate peace. But whenever his army outnumbered the enemy, he would attack all at once. He would usually attack with a force 10 times larger than the enemy's. This was the strategy he used, for example, when he attacked Odawara Castle. With this strategy, he could deprive the enemy of the will to fight, which enabled him to win without a fight and minimize his own losses.

Fighting an enemy of equal size leads to tremendous losses. For example, a battle of 10,000 soldiers against 12,000 soldiers will result in significant casualties on both sides. On the other hand, a battle of 10,000 soldiers against 100,000 soldiers will sap the smaller army's will to fight. Because the smaller army can see that they have no chance of winning, they will surrender without even going into battle. This is the strategy for the strong.

In general, whether an organization is strong or weak depends on its size, but it can also depend on the field it is competing in. You need to keep this in mind.

2

The Strategy to Survive and Win in the Market

What led Nobunaga Oda to win the Battle of Okehazama?

When you plan your strategy, you must not overestimate your ability. It is better to assume that your ability is limited and there is a limit to what you can do. You should think of ways to succeed with these limitations in mind. People who incorrectly believe they have overwhelming abilities cannot develop good strategies.

Let us learn from Nobunaga Oda (1534 - 1582), another Japanese feudal lord. What do you think led him to win the Battle of Okehazama in 1560? This has long been a historic theme of research for many historians. Nevertheless, the battle tactic Nobunaga employed was not his own invention but a strategy used since ancient times. He attacked the enemy forces that were centrally positioned, which was a common approach in military strategy when fighting against a large army. When an army becomes excessively large, there tend to be delays in the commander's orders reaching everyone because the distance between the head and the rear of the army becomes larger. By attacking the centrally positioned enemy forces in a long line of troops, you can split the army in half and throw it into confusion and disarray before they even realize what has happened.

It is said that Yoshimoto Imagawa (1519 - 1560), the commander of the enemy forces, led 30,000 men at the time, while Nobunaga only had 2,000 or 3,000 men. Nobunaga faced an enemy force that was 10 times the size of his own army and needed to figure out a way to defeat it. Yoshimoto's men were marching up the Tokaido Road, but because it was not a well-maintained road, they had to travel in a long line. You can probably imagine just how stretched out a line of 30,000 troops would be. When Yoshimoto and his men were resting at Okehazama, Nobunaga ambushed Yoshimoto. Only 300 soldiers were said to have been with Yoshimoto at the time, so it was only natural that Nobunaga's army of 2,000 won. He was meant to win.

In battle strategy, attacking your enemy's forces that are centrally positioned is the golden rule. A large army may appear strong, but they are only strong when fighting an all-out battle on open, flat land. They are vulnerable if they are attacked while crossing a river, too. If they are attacked when only half of their troops have crossed the river, they will be split in half and thrown into chaos.

Applying this golden rule of battle strategy to company management

You can apply the idea of attacking the enemy's centrally positioned forces to modern-day company management. Large companies typically operate their businesses on a large scale, which resembles an extended military formation. It often becomes difficult for them to devise strategies for specific aspects of their business. Because of this, they can be defeated when their most vulnerable core is attacked.

Take, for example, a leading Japanese supermarket. They once implemented a discount strategy but were eventually defeated by a new supermarket. The reason for their defeat lies in their strategy of over-diversification. When a company tries to expand its scope of business, the CEO cannot keep a close eye on each and every market it has entered. That is why they will be defeated if another company initiates a full-force attack focused on a particular area, which can be seen in some large supermarkets and department stores that are in decline. In fact, they are being defeated by convenience stores and other small shops that use a small-destroyer-style strategy and make targeted attacks. Small stores like these are doing very well now. Nevertheless, because they still carry hundreds of different products, even more specialized businesses focus on selling hamburgers or rice bowls at lower prices, for example. These specialized shops may challenge these stores in the bento lunch market and win against them by focusing on a narrower niche.

When your business grows large, you must adopt the strategies that are appropriate for large companies, but until then, you need to focus your energy on a specific area; otherwise, you will not be able to win. No matter how large your competitors may be, they cannot be equally strong in all markets they have entered. So, by concentrating your forces on your competitor's weakest areas and specializing in that field, you will be able to defeat your competitor in that particular market.

3
Company Management During a Recession

1) Focus your company's forces on its strengths

Here, let me discuss what management should keep in mind during a recession. In an economic downturn, it is essential to reduce staffing and expenses in departments that are in the red or underperforming, while further strengthening those that are doing well. Having said that, some deficits can be considered "healthy and positive"—deficits created by departments that show great potential for future growth. Although they are in the red now, they have the potential to succeed and become the main revenue-producing departments in two or three years' time. You must not give up on these promising departments, which will most certainly generate profit in the future, but rather, continue investing in them until they bear fruit. This is known as anticipatory investment. On the other hand, you need to downsize departments that are structurally unprofitable and reallocate their budget and staffing to profitable departments.

Making investments during a recession requires great expertise, so generally, it is risky to invest more than 20 percent of a company's total revenue. You need to keep this in mind at all times. By wanting more than you deserve, you could lead your company into bankruptcy, putting many employees out of work. Therefore, business owners must always stay grounded. They cannot expect to be successful all the time.

Company owners are usually full of ideas and, in the beginning, they take on new challenges one after another. However, not all of them can continue to succeed. The people who can maintain their businesses after reaching a certain level of success are those who shift their mindset to one of avoiding losing battles. A business owner must be able to determine what not to do. There are buds of success in some decisions that appear to be taking a step backward or being passive. You should stop making wasteful capital investments and staff allocations, and call off high-risk plans. Instead, focus your energy on the departments that are making steady profits. This is a very important way of thinking, much like pruning a shrub. People often become preoccupied with their immediate interests and end up delving into too many things, so you need to be careful not to fall into the same trap.

Extending your line of troops will put them in danger, no matter how big your army is; you will not be able to win if battles break out on multiple fronts. You can defeat the enemy by deploying elite troops in one location and having them all fight at once, but if they are scattered across a wide area, they will become weak despite having been strong initially. To be victorious, you need to concentrate your forces under the leadership of an outstanding commander and make a breakthrough at a critical point. When there are multiple opponents, the best strategy is to fight them one by one. You must win each battle using your entire army. Win one battle at a time before moving on to the next.

2) Strengthen your company's management structure for the future

Another essential point to consider during a recession is how to improve the quality of your company's management. Company owners tend to be very careless during economic booms; they spend money like water, especially on things like advertising and customer entertainment. But instead, during a recession, companies should work on raising the quality of their management. The first thing they should do is reduce unnecessary expenditure and find ways to operate with lower costs.

They also need to distinguish between employees who are a liability and those who are not. During a recession, companies should identify valuable workers who are truly contributing to making profits.

3) Invest in your human resources

It is also essential to invest in human resources by educating and training employees. Once the economy improves, businesses will expand rapidly, so company owners need to prepare and educate their employees for when that time comes. This may not immediately generate revenue for the company, but they must educate their employees well and build up strength they can use in the future. I strongly encourage companies to build their inner strength by making these kinds of efforts during a recession.

During a recession or a slump, both companies and individuals must restrict their activities and focus their energy on fewer things. The key is not to disperse your energy too widely. Gather and conserve your energy, and use it on what matters most for making a breakthrough. This is the key to achieving success.

4

Important Preparations in Times of Success

Three points to consider during a period of development

Every organization or business goes through a period of development. During a development period, everything that the business does generally turns out well. However, we live in a surprisingly well-balanced world where no one business or industry can continue to perform extraordinarily well for decades. There is a rise and fall of companies that is said to occur in 30-year cycles; there are similar cycles in work as well. Therefore, the following points should be considered when your business is growing.

First, focus on developing your business as much as possible and aim to achieve the greatest possible growth during a period of development, because it will not last forever. I recommend that you seize the opportunity for further growth and focus on expanding your business as much as possible while you can. This is the first piece of wisdom that you need if you are aiming to attain infinite development.

Second, during the growth period, consider how to diversify your business. A business experiencing rapid growth usually has a blockbuster product or a lucrative revenue stream. So, you should use it as leverage to open new possibilities and sow seeds for the next development, which you will be able to reap the benefit of in five, ten, or twenty years' time. In other words, you should make secure investments that will generate returns for your company in the future. Even if it does not bring you immediate returns, you should think in terms of investments that will yield profits in a few years' time.

The third piece of wisdom for achieving infinite development is to have a contingency plan to ensure your business survives if the current situation or the environment you are operating in changes completely. When a business is doing well, it can be quite difficult to imagine this, but you must consider how many years your company could endure if it experiences its biggest crisis ever. It is essential to develop a concrete plan for how to survive in dire situations like this.

How to survive in an ever-changing environment

Even a company that has constantly generated large profits by exporting cars could find itself in serious trouble if foreign importers start shutting out their products and they lose their sales channels. If that occurs, it will probably try to survive by seeking sales channels in other countries or by manufacturing its cars overseas. But it should also think about what it would do if people stopped buying cars altogether. The very product that brought about the company's growth can suddenly become completely worthless. Therefore, you need to consider what you will do if the cause of the current development is no longer there. That is, a car company needs to consider not only what will happen if they can no longer sell their cars in particular countries like the U.S. or the U.K., but also what will happen if people stop driving cars, and they can no longer be sold to anyone.

To avoid a crisis, you sometimes need to have a completely different perspective. In addition to thinking about making investments for the future, you should also think about what people will need if your company's products stop selling. For example, automobile manufacturers might imagine that the modes of transport in the future could be some kind of aircraft, or a vehicle that travels at extremely high speeds on ground, below the ground, or on water. They must then consider whether they have the potential to enter a new market when airplanes become more accessible to consumers, or when other high-speed vehicles that travel on water, above ground, or underground are developed. You need to create a survival plan in case the main reason for your current business growth starts working against you.

5
Winning Under Any Circumstances

1) Market segmentation

The basic way to conduct marketing or pioneer a new market is to discover people's needs. Figuring out what people need is the foundation of marketing. Nevertheless, it can be quite difficult to identify people's needs when there are already many similar products or companies out there. When people's needs are already satisfied, you must create a new need. To do this, you need to be creative in finding and developing better techniques, superior products, or other goods that will make people's lives more convenient. Therefore, marketing is not merely about discovering needs but also about developing and creating new needs.

Marketing, in the truest sense, does not mean producing goods that cater equally to everyone. A long time ago, the American automaker Ford came out with its black Model T and started mass producing it with exactly the same color and shape. This enabled them to lower the price of the car and make it affordable even for the average worker. Henry Ford forged a new era in this way and made a fortune, but his company eventually lost to GM (General Motors).

Why did the automaker Ford lose to GM? In fact, the very thing that led to its success also became the cause of its failure. Ford managed to reduce prices by mass-producing identical cars, but as more people started driving the same black Model Ts, it became difficult to tell them apart because they were all the same color and shape. Their license plates were the only thing that distinguished one from another. Because of this, people grew bored with the black Model T. But manufacturing cars in different colors, such as red, blue, and white, would complicate the assembly line and increase costs, which was why Ford had seen so much success by standardizing and mass-producing cars. Their goal was to make cars cheap and affordable for people on average salaries. However, this very goal then became the reason for their defeat. Once GM began making cars aimed at different social classes, Ford could not compete and ultimately lost.

This example shows that something that once led you to success can later become the cause of your defeat. You cannot take over market share unless you standardize your product and mass-produce it. But if you want to outdo companies with a large market share, you should go for the market that is not covered by standardized products. That is, you should target customers who are dissatisfied with the standardized products. This is called segmentation—you divide the market into smaller groups and focus on a specific target. This is how you can form a new market by discovering and creating new needs.

2) Innovation

Another important factor is innovation, but how should we understand it? The economist Joseph Schumpeter defined it as "the combination of heterogeneous elements," which is certainly one way to look at it. Innovation can happen when you produce something new by combining things of a different nature. On the other hand, management consultant Peter Drucker defined innovation in a different way. He said that, contrary to what people think, innovation is not about creating something new. Rather, conventional methods and systems inevitably become obsolete, so a time will come when you have to abandon the ways of doing things that once brought you good results. But it is not enough to abandon just one way; you have to scrap the whole system you have been using until now. This systematic abandonment is what innovation is all about, according to Drucker.

Recently, the role of government offices has been discussed in Japan. I think it is time for the central government to systematically abolish a lot of its ministries and agencies. They need to think thoroughly about what to scrap entirely, rather than just adjusting or altering certain parts. They need to look at their work from the perspective of whether it is truly necessary or can be eliminated altogether. There is likely to be a tremendous amount of unnecessary work going on, which is mostly hindering private companies from proceeding with their work. The government-led efforts worked well when Japan was rising from the ashes of World War II, but now that the private sector has grown large, the various rules and regulations requiring official approval are significantly hindering its work. That is why innovation is required now. Because Japanese citizens are sensing this, they are expressing their strong dissatisfaction with government offices. The government is unequivocally in the wrong for trying to raise taxes when it hinders the private sector and practices poor management.

When you feel you have reached a limit, constantly think about how to make a breakthrough and achieve further progress. Innovation comes with pain. Innovation urges you to abandon what was effective in the past, so pain is inevitable. Even so, if you want to continue developing your company, you must undergo this "surgery" at some point.

3) An Invincible Culture

Once you have achieved a certain level of success, you then need to think about how to keep succeeding. Building a system that helps you stay victorious is important for both individuals and organizations. Even if you happen to succeed, generally speaking, it will not last long, because all things are impermanent. To keep winning, you need extensive preparation, and you need to constantly think of ways to stay victorious.

To be more specific, you either need to be resourceful or have ample resources to keep fighting again and again. For instance, if you, as an individual, succeed in creating a product that becomes a big hit, you then need to think about how to keep creating new hit products, year after year. You need to think about what to do the following year, the year after that, or even 10 years later. This is also true for an organization. As your company achieves success, you need to think about how to keep succeeding.

A system that allows you to keep winning may take the form of a company policy, but I think it also comes in the form of a culture that continually innovates. An individual, as well as an organization, must keep innovating and constantly think of creative ways to build new strategies. There is a world of difference between those who have aspired to develop this kind of system and those who have not; people's lives and organizations' strategies will differ greatly. Usually, people are not aware of this difference and tend to think that they were just lucky if they won or unlucky if they lost. But truly strong individuals and organizations strive enthusiastically to create a system that helps them keep winning.

It is essential that you first consider how to create a system like this. Always think about how to keep winning. Then, you will find hints or wisdom welling up from within you, and you will come to understand what you need to prepare for the future.

CHAPTER ELEVEN

Providing Better Training for Your Employees

1
Do You Believe That People Can Grow Through Education?

The key to success in business lies in nurturing your personnel. As long as you can do this, other issues, such as money problems, will naturally be resolved. Therefore, you must first bring out the best in the people who work for you now. To do that, it is essential that you believe in the effect of education and believe that people will undeniably grow and do better through education. This belief is similar to having faith in God.

Are you able to believe that instructing and guiding people will definitely help them grow and that they will sooner or later produce good results? Are you able to believe that your efforts to nurture them will surely lead them to become better? Whether you believe this or not will be the difference between becoming a true success or a failure. If you do not, it means you lack the qualities to be a leader. You would be better off focusing on refining your special skills in a particular field of expertise. It would be best for you to make the most of your strengths and become a specialist rather than a generalist. On the other hand, if you are able to believe that people will unquestionably do better through education or guidance, you should aspire to walk the road to becoming a generalist and a manager. Figuring out which category you fall into is part of achieving great success.

2

Learning from *The Records of the Three Kingdoms*

Yuan Shao did not listen to his military advisor

Let us look at two leaders from the Chinese classic, *The Records of the Three Kingdoms*, to learn more about leadership. In the age of the Three Kingdoms, there was the Yellow Turban Rebellion, which threw the country into chaos. Rival warlords rose to defend and expand their territories, giving rise to many heroes who aspired to unify the country, and in the process, they formed and broke alliances with one another. Among them was Yuan Shao, a powerful warlord in North China at the time. He fought against Cao Cao, who would later become the King of Wei. It is said that Yuan Shao had a large army of 700,000 soldiers while Cao Cao had just 70,000. Under normal circumstances, Cao Cao would not have had a chance of winning, but he managed to defeat Yuan Shao's army in the well-known Battle of Guandu in 200 AD. This victory completely changed Chinese history.

During the battle, Yuan Shao's strategist offered various kinds of advice, but Yuan did not listen to him. He even sent his strategist to prison when he suggested an idea that was different from his own. Eventually, Yuan suffered a tremendous loss that meant his army was nearly annihilated, and then returned home. Upon hearing about his return, the prison guard said to the strategist, "Good for you. Now that your advice was proven to be right, you should soon be released," but the strategist responded, "So, Yuan Shao lost the battle? Then, he will have my head." Sure enough, when Yuan Shao returned, he executed the strategist who gave him the right advice.

This was how Yuan Shao used his men. He would simply kill people who opposed his ideas or proposed different ideas because he felt that they were pointing out his mistakes. This is very similar to how Hitler behaved. Leaders like that will ultimately suffer defeat even if they are powerful for a certain period of time because people will soon lose trust in them.

Cao Cao, who recruited talented men

In comparison, Cao Cao of the Kingdom of Wei had a strong desire to recruit talented people. He recruited many military generals and also gathered many strategists by paying them his utmost respect. This is why the Kingdom of Shu, under the strategist Zhuge Liang, could not defeat the Kingdom of Wei, no matter how hard they tried. Part of the reason why

Shu could not beat Wei was that their economy was one-fifth the size of Wei's economy, but the main reason for their defeat was that Cao Cao had laid strong foundations in Wei by gathering plenty of talented people.

Cao Cao's character was the reason behind Wei's plentiful talent. He was a strong military general himself, and was also an excellent strategist. Talented people typically tend to dislike other talented people, but Cao Cao actively sought them out, even though he himself was so gifted that he could write a textbook on military strategy. That is why Wei was full of talented people.

Meanwhile, in the Kingdom of Shu, only Zhuge Liang stood out as a military advisor, which means they probably had no other capable military advisors. Shu also had some outstanding military heroes like Guan Yu and Zhang Fei. But if you think about it now, the fact that no particular individual stood out in Wei means that it had many military heroes. So, it is clear that Cao Cao was extremely talented at mobilizing their army to fight wars. With numerous advisors and generals at his command, he was able to dispatch them one after another into the battlefield, allowing him to fight battles indefinitely.

Even though Cao Cao lost many battles, he would always bounce back. Even after the terrible defeat in the Battle of the Red Cliffs, he did not fall. He had the strength to bounce back no matter how many times he was defeated. This was possible because of his desire to recruit talented people. Nowadays, Cao Cao is known as a cunning hero with a bad reputation, but perhaps he was the real hero in *The Records of the Three Kingdoms*. While Zhuge Liang and Liu Bei are very popular today, there is another way to look at Zhuge Liang. It was Zhuge Liang's idea to divide the land into three parts, but doing so invited many unnecessary wars and ultimately led Shu to be destroyed during the age of its next leader. From this, we could say that if it were not for Zhuge Liang's idea to divide the land into three parts, Cao Cao could have unified the land, and therefore, Zhuge Liang was a hindrance to unification. We could say that Zhuge Liang lacked ability in this sense.

3

Creating an Organization That Evaluates Strong "Genes"

There is no development in an organization driven by jealousy

I would like to mention the merit-based human resources system as one of the key aspects of management that is related to innovation. Traditional organizations usually have an established pyramid-type hierarchy and system of values. But when you start a new type of business and try to develop it, the qualities required of your employees will change rapidly. The abilities they need and the results they are expected to achieve will change frequently. A magnificent achievement this year may be considered mundane next year. A capable leader this year may not be evaluated so highly the following year. This only happens in companies that are developing; companies that are not developing do not experience this.

Companies that see no growth are basically the same as stagnant societies or agricultural societies, where "a nail that sticks out gets hammered down." In these kinds of societies, people avoid standing out and instead value community life. Therefore, societies that are not developing can easily become societies driven by jealousy; anyone who dares to stand out is immediately brought down. A stagnant society places heavy emphasis on equality, which can result in an extremely jealous society that does not allow anyone to stand out. This is because aiming for progress leads to disparity, making it difficult to strike a balance between the two. In a jealousy-driven society where a culture of envying successful people is prevalent, any attempt to make progress will most likely be hindered.

It is essential to develop a culture that celebrates successful people. The U.S. is ahead of Japan in this regard. In the U.S., people respect individuals or companies that have attained success. They probably believe successful people are emitting a particular kind of aura. In Japan, on the other hand, living an average life without achieving great success or standing out is considered more important. People try to avoid becoming a threat to their superiors because they know that this type of attitude is more pleasing to their superiors. But if the culture is left this way, employees who please their superiors despite being incompetent will gradually climb the corporate ladder because of the seniority system, whereas competent employees will be sidelined for being too outspoken. If an organization has grown large with many superiors who try to promote incompetent subordinates, it will start to decline. This always happens. By the time the organization is on its last legs, only sycophants, the mediocre, and the harmless will have been promoted.

Consider work itself to be the reward for your achievements

In a well-run organization, "strong genes," or competent workers, are highly valued. These strong genes will influence other genes to become stronger; in other words, competent workers will inspire other employees to become more capable. It is vital that these "competent genes" are passed from one employee to another. Instead of regarding strong genes as a foreign substance that needs to be eliminated, you need to create a culture in which others become "infected" and develop strong genes themselves. A company that nurtures this culture will become a robust organization with a progress-oriented mindset.

Therefore, companies should adopt a merit-based human resources system that is not necessarily associated with job titles. I believe that work itself is the reward for your achievements. Titles and salaries are merely the results, or the residues, of work. Those who are competent will attract work, and work itself is the reward for their achievements. This idea is essential.

CHAPTER TWELVE

Gaining Support from the Invisible World

1
Receiving Help from Your Guardian and Guiding Spirits

Just having earthly power and abilities is not enough to make you successful. It has been confirmed that power from the invisible world is clearly at work, so why not use it? Everyone has a guardian spirit, and if you work in a specialized field, spirits of a higher level—also known as guiding spirits—that are most appropriate for your occupation may come to help you too. There are countless guiding spirits in heaven, and when someone in this world is given a position they deserve, they will start to receive guidance from spirits suited to their level of expertise. You should receive guidance from these spirits, because if you do, you will be able to make spectacular achievements at work.

As you work hard, you will be able to tell for yourself when you are being guided. To receive power from your guardian and guiding spirits, you need to maintain a pure and humble attitude. If you selflessly and humbly strive to embody the power of God or Buddha in this world, you will gradually find that the power of the heavenly guidance you receive will double. On the contrary, if you let clouds develop over your mind and live egotistically, your guardian and guiding spirits will drift away from you. Just as you would not want to stay around egotistic people, neither do the spirits in heaven. Because they are particularly sensitive to the spiritual vibrations of people's minds, they find egotistic people unpleasant and try to avoid them. Some guardian spirits may even give up on the people they are guiding and abandon them as if to say, "If that's what you want to do, then so be it." Then, those people may end up attracting evil spirits that emit similar vibrations.

We could call people who are possessed by evil spirits "bad people," but nonetheless, even bad people can be successful in this world. If they strongly focus their will on achieving a specific goal and push forward aggressively, they may be able to enjoy some degree of success. However, their reputation will rarely last long in this world, let alone in the afterlife. In most cases, people who are possessed by evil spirits will be disliked by others or will have a bad reputation, which will make them feel lonely, sad, and dissatisfied in their hearts. Many of them become unhappy in their twilight years.

Those who aim to become successful through burglary will attract many spirits who once lived as thieves in their past lives; the vibrations of their minds will attract like-minded spirits. On the other hand, if you make efforts earnestly, selflessly, and open-mindedly with high aspirations, you will be able to receive guidance from heaven. Therefore, whenever you find that a path has opened before you through hard work, you should always be grateful for the guidance you were given, even if you cannot see the spirits who helped you. Express gratitude in your heart, such as "Thank you, my guardian spirit. Thank you, my guiding spirits." Then, they will be pleased and will help you even more.

2

The Power of Visualization Will Drastically Change Your Surroundings

Set a goal based on your ideals or your convictions

Once you have solidified your ideals or convictions, you will next need to set a goal to realize them. Once a goal is set, individuals and groups will strive to achieve it.

The purer your desire to realize your ideal image is, the stronger your conviction and determination to realize it will be. A halfhearted desire indicates a lack of determination to realize your ideal. It is the same as an incompetent employee thinking they couldn't care less whether or not their product sells. Both company owners and employees should think, "Our product is really excellent and will benefit people around the world. If it spreads, people and society will have much to gain. That's why we aspire to increase our sales." Only then can they properly set their company's sales quota, and each salesperson can then set their own quota accordingly.

So first, set a clear direction and establish an ideal to aim for. Without it, your work is just for fun and not professional work, whether it is a religious activity or a business activity.

It is important to set yourself a goal based on your ideals or convictions.

Clearly visualize yourself achieving your goal

After you have set yourself a goal, visualize yourself achieving it with as much detail as possible. You must vividly envision yourself achieving your goal one year or ten years from now. Then, engrave that image deep in your mind, again and again.

Once you have clearly set your future vision, the earthly world—also known as the Phenomenal World—will work to realize it. Your own will or willpower will work toward achieving it, and your guardian spirit and various guiding spirits will also come to help you. What is more, your strong willpower will influence the people you are working with. It will not only affect them spiritually but will also affect their guardian and guiding spirits. When people see you working with conviction, they will be moved, and gradually, a network of various types of people will form around you, which will help you to succeed. They will consider your words and ideals to be like divine revelations and will be magnetized to you.

Accept the image of your ideals being realized

Where does the power to attract people come from? It comes from visualizing and accepting a clear image of your ideals being realized. Suppose you run a business that generates one million dollars in annual sales and say that you eventually want to develop it into a 100-million-dollar company. There is a significant difference in scale between a million-dollar company and a 100-million-dollar company. The difference is a hundredfold. If you are merely expressing your ideals, saying that you want to become a 100-million-dollar company, and are unable to imagine what would happen when it actually comes true, you will miss the chance to achieve it.

A million-dollar company has its own management style, operating style, and decision-making process suited to its scale, which differ from those of a 100-million-dollar company or a billion-dollar company. So, you need to be able to visualize what will happen when your company reaches that size. For example, you must be able to clearly visualize in your mind, "When our company reaches 100 million dollars in annual sales, we will have this many factories and this many salespeople. We will have branches in these areas and hire this many employees in total. We will be getting loans of these amounts from the bank and be putting this much effort into advertising." If you are unable to visualize this, your company will most likely remain at its current size.

A CEO with the mindset of a million-dollar company president will only be able to manage a company of that size and will only be able to grow in line with GDP. What I mean is that, if GDP growth is zero percent, the company will have zero percent growth; if it is negative, the company will have negative growth; and if it is three percent, the company will grow by three percent. A company like this will continue to grow at a rate similar to GDP. Of course, even if you are not able to visualize your company growing larger than its current size, you can still find happiness in maintaining it where it is. But if you can clearly visualize and believe that your company will become a 10-million, 100-million, or a billion-dollar company, and if you are confident that it will lead to many people's happiness, and you feel a strong sense of mission and conviction to achieve that goal, then you should picture all of the details in your mind. You need to accept this image and work on visualizing yourself having achieved your goal.

The snake that cannot shed its skin has to die

As you continue to accept the ideal image of your company, you will gradually think in ways that are appropriate to managing the level of business that your company is aiming toward. On the other hand, people who cannot adjust their thinking to match the level of management required will not be able to develop their business further. A business will not grow beyond its CEO's capacity. To use hermit crabs as an example, they need to leave their old shell to be able to grow further. They need to change to a bigger shell because, if they remain in the same one, they will not be able to grow beyond its size. As the saying goes, "The snake that cannot shed its skin has to die." In the same way, you have to change how you think and act as your business develops.

To do this, you need to set a goal and picture in your mind an image of your ideal result. If you are unable to visualize it, or to put it another way, if you are afraid of what would happen if it comes true, you will not be able to accept it.

3

Be Humble and Receive the Energy of Wealth from the Great Universe

God's energy is flowing toward you

The great universe is overflowing with magnificent energy, although it may be invisible. It is indeed magnificent; it is the power that brings about development and forever makes people happy. It is also filled with creativity and love. This invisible power flows through "pipes" or "blood vessels" to all beings in the entire universe. These invisible, slim pipes reach the heart of each and every individual. Just as water pipes extend into every home, the energy of the great universe pours powerfully into the heart of each and every person.

You can control this energy in a similar way to how you use a tap; turn it on to let the water run, and turn it off to stop the water from running. This is how it works. If you hold a certain state of mind, the energy of love will flow abundantly through the pipes of the great universe into you, while other kinds of thoughts stop it from flowing.

Then, what kind of thoughts should we have? Interestingly, if you try to turn on the tap for your own sake, the water will run for a while, but before long, it will naturally stop. On the other hand, if you teach others how to turn on the tap, a spring of energy will gush forth endlessly, like an inexhaustible well. This is one of the wonders of the universe.

How to receive God's energy

What I am trying to say here is very simple. The more you attune the vibration of your mind to that of God or the Primordial Buddha, the happier you will be. It is as simple as that. There are particular "radio waves" transmitted by God, and you can receive them by tuning in to those frequencies.

What kinds of waves are being transmitted from God's radio station? They are, for example, love, wisdom, courage, justice, hope, joy, freedom, equality, fairness, and progress. God's radio waves are full of these energies. If you make an effort to attune your mind to these wavelengths—and just by doing so—you can receive God's light indefinitely. Acquiring the ability to do this is virtually the same as gaining infinite wealth.

First, you must have a righteous heart. Be the kind of person who loathes evil and loves justice. Know that love is universal and is of the greatest value in this world. Then, affirm that wealth manifests to bring prosperity to this world, and understand that the happiness of all humanity serves as the foundation for your own happiness to grow and expand. Moreover, you must awaken more to your mission to live for the benefit of the public. Instead of confining yourself to your own small shell, develop the mindset to build a happy society with many people. Utopia will be realized only when people who wish for it work together.

Open up your heart and receive God's energy. Embrace the ideals of God as they are. Receive the energy of God without blocking it with human perceptions. This is the attitude you need to have.

If you want to receive the energy of God, pray with a pure and innocent heart. Remove any wrong or negative thoughts from your mind, and pray wholeheartedly to God.

Lord
Please grant me
A drop of wisdom
From the great ocean of wisdom you possess

Lord
Please grant me
A drop of love
From the great ocean of love you possess

Lord
Please grant me
A drop of wealth
From the great ocean of wealth you possess

Lord
Please grant me
A drop of mercy
From the great ocean of mercy you possess

This is how you should pray. God is infinite; God is the power that makes everything possible. Your worries will dissolve with just a single drop of God's power. What is more, many angels are working hard in the other world, or the Real World, as well as in this world, to help grant all the wishes that people on earth make to God. When you pray, light of angels that incarnated in this world will come to help you, and light of angels in heaven will also start working to help you.

4

Empty Your Mind and Entrust Yourself to a Greater Power

The true meaning behind not being able to achieve your dreams

When you are feeling like you are at the end of your rope, please use prayer. I recommend that you pray wholeheartedly. Sometimes, your prayers will be granted, but at other times, they will not. When your prayers are not granted, it means there is something off with your prayers—it could be that the content is inappropriate or the timing is not right.

When you think that your wish to become a certain way accords with the Will of God or Buddha, you can pray for it to come true, but when your prayer is not granted as you had expected, it can mean that another will is at work from a grander perspective. In that case, you need to be obedient and accept the Divine Will, because there are many factors that cannot be seen from the limited perspective of this world. There are an infinite number of cases where dreams are not realized as we wish. We must always be willing to accept the heavenly judgment that is made from a grander perspective when it says, "It is better for this not to happen now. At this moment in time, it is better for this wish not to be granted."

The greatest unhappiness can turn into happiness

Sometimes, we can avoid experiencing unhappiness or enjoy prolonged happiness by having our wish not come true. This is something we will not understand unless we can see ourselves from a far-distant perspective. So, it is wrong to curse God or Buddha for not having our prayers granted. I would especially like to remind you of the importance of this point.

This is what I actually experienced. I often experienced that things did not go as I had expected, and I was forced to change the direction I was heading in. However, looking at the overall course of events, I now feel that things ultimately unfolded according to my wishes. There was a general flow of fate from which I could not escape.

If I look at the details, there were so many times when things did not go as I wanted. Sometimes, the door that takes you in a certain direction closes, but this can lead to other opportunities that enable you to fulfill your mission or heaven's will. We may not understand or accept this at the time. It is usually a sad thing for a door to close, and at the time, we may not be able to see that it is leading us to our next mission. But you need to know that what you think of as your greatest unhappiness could be your source of happiness later on.

Become one with your deep consciousness and awaken to your mission

People think at different levels of their consciousness; some of their thoughts take place deep in their consciousness, while others take place in the surface-level consciousness. Among the wishes that are made in our surface consciousness, many are better not to be realized.

All we can do is entrust the great flow of our fate to heaven's will. People suffer whenever something unfortunate happens, but I get the impression that the majority of their suffering is not worth the pain they go through. It is difficult to see the great flow of fate. While it is good to diligently make efforts to achieve your goal, at the same time, you must also become one with your deep consciousness. For this reason, I recommend that you repeatedly meditate deeply to realize your hopes at places like Happy Science shojas. Because your surface consciousness is limited to you, yourself, only, in many cases, the goal that you believe to be the realization of the Truth is nothing more than a worldly delusion or desire. So you need to meditate repeatedly to see if your goal is in line with the consciousness that lies deep in your mind.

A wish will eventually fade away and disappear unless it comes from deep within. At that time, the right path may clearly open up for you. In the beginning, you may strive to achieve it self-centeredly, but as you move forward on the path to realize your dream, you will increasingly feel like entrusting the result to something greater. You will feel the work of Outside Power more strongly. When you feel that you are living to fulfill your mission, you will no longer have doubts about what you must do. When you are wavering between your desires and struggling to achieve them, in most cases, you will still be confined to your egoism and selfishness. When you truly find your calling, you will hardly ever doubt yourself. For this reason, it is important to awaken to your holy mission, or a public duty or public mission, from a broader perspective.

CHAPTER THIRTEEN

A Willingness to Contribute to Others and Society

1

A Win-Win Approach Taught in Buddhism

Always be willing to live for the sake of others

It is essential not to keep all your success to yourself when you are walking the road to becoming a success. I am not saying that wanting to be promoted to section manager, department manager, or executive in a company, for example, is wrong; you can certainly aspire to be one. I understand that it would be very painful and discouraging if you could never gain any recognition or respect from others despite your hard work. It is good to have the desire to be promoted so that you can work continuously for many decades. However, as you make your way up to section manager, department manager, or executive positions, you should not use your work and aspirations solely to achieve your own success. Instead of focusing 100 percent on yourself, you must, at the very least, spare some energy for others. If you have a one-liter bottle, for example, do not fill it all for yourself but instead leave a little room for other things, even if it is just 100 or 200 milliliters. As you make your way to department manager, for instance, you should help others succeed as well by assisting them with their work, promoting them, or sharing your insights with them on how to become successful. By wishing good luck to other people, you will be able to gain support and approval from many people.

Those who are on the path to success will inevitably become the target of strong envy and jealousy from other people, which cannot be completely avoided. If you are not successful, people do not get jealous of you. No one feels jealous of those who are failing, so if you become the target of other people's jealousy, it is a sign that you are succeeding. Therefore, you must more or less accept the fact that jealousy from other people is inevitable. Still, when you find yourself in a position that attracts jealousy from others, you should always be willing to live for the sake of others. While you do not need to show it, you must constantly keep it in your mind.

Can you wish for other people's success?

When other people achieve greater success than you, perhaps you, too, may become competitive and jealous of them. If that happens, you must make an effort to restrain those feelings as much as possible and instead try to praise their success, even if it goes against your true feelings. Tell them, "That's so wonderful!" and congratulate them on their success. For example, when you see other companies expanding their businesses more than yours, do not be jealous and say, "They were just lucky. Things worked out for them purely by chance." Instead, congratulate them and say, "That's wonderful. I hope our company will follow suit and succeed, too."

As the saying goes, curses return upon the heads of those who curse. If you wish for the unhappiness or failure of others, your narrow-minded heart will ultimately attract failure to yourself as well. You, too, would not feel so inclined to cheer on, assist, or applaud someone who wants others to fail. Instead, you will want to support someone who wants others to be happy. The same is true for companies. If the success of one company brings unhappiness to other companies, you will not want to support it. It is good for a company to grow, of course, but the condition for continued success is that its CEO and employees want to make a positive impact on the industry as a whole so that the country or world will prosper.

That is why it is essential to control your selfish desires. The attitude of wishing for other people's success may make you seem naive, but controlling your selfish desires, rather than completely following them, will eventually help you gain support from many people and earn greater happiness and success.

The universal law taught in Buddhism

Buddhism teaches the law of causality, which comprises two elements: time causality and space causality. Time causality represents a vertical relationship in which a cause leads to a result. Based on this idea, good deeds yield good results while bad deeds yield bad results. In other words, acts that benefit others will eventually lead to good results over time, while deeds that harm others will lead you to pay the price at some point. This is the general understanding of the law of causality.

But there is another aspect to it, which is what I call space causality. Space causality represents a horizontal relationship between people or between you and the world. This idea shows that we human beings are not living alone. According to one interpretation, the Japanese character for "person" (人) symbolizes bundles of harvested wheat straws or sheaves of rice supporting each other to stand upright. It is indeed true that human beings depend on each other to live; husbands and wives, parents and children, brothers and sisters, friends, and acquaintances all support each other to live. We, humans, cannot live alone. We can live because we support each other. When things start to go well for a person and their cogwheel of life starts turning for the better, other cogwheels that are connected to it will also turn for the better. Imagine a family with a husband, a wife, and their children. If the father succeeds at his job, his wife and children will also become happier. This happiness will then spread further to others. In this way, people exist based on mutual relationships with one another.

We are all living in a world of mutual influence

Your personal improvement will lead to the improvement of others and also lead to the development of your company, your society, your country, and eventually the world. It is also true that, when someone else becomes better, it will affect others, including you.

The growth of a company will lead to the happiness of its employees as well. But if the company is on the verge of bankruptcy, its employees will not be rewarded for their work, no matter how hard they try. Even if a company has some outstanding employees, it will not do any better when the company is going under. There are times when the whole industry suffers a recession, and at such times, many companies in the industry will undergo bankruptcy or M&A. There is not much that can be done in these circumstances. Further, companies can be affected by the societal environment and the country's policies. Whether a company is being run in a free market economy, in a communist country, or under a military dictatorship will also have an effect on it.

Therefore, it is important to recognize and hold the worldview that we all influence one another as we live in this world; not only are we affected by others, but we also affect other people.

2
Winning People's Trust and Their "Faith" in You

Your goal should be social contribution and public interest

Companies uphold the pursuit of profit as their primary goal. The mission of a stock corporation, for example, is to increase profit and pay dividends to its shareholders because shareholders' investments are what keep the business running. In Japan, companies tend to value their employees, but in Western countries, companies value their shareholders because there is a strong belief that they are the ones who truly own companies. Of course, companies strive to increase their profit for the sake of their employees, but they also do so to pay dividends to their shareholders. Companies need to reward the shareholders who have trusted and invested in them. For this reason, it is very important for companies to generate profits.

But some companies do not stop there and instead start working for social contribution or public interest. These companies will gradually have a strong spiritual field form around them, as religions do. This spiritual field represents the credibility of those companies, that is, people's trust in the companies' goodwill. People will say, for example, "This company's service is trustworthy," "I can trust the aspirations of the people working for this company," "They always think about what is best for us," "They are professional, so there is no need to worry," or "The medical service of this hospital is of the highest level." These companies will begin to function like a religion and take on religion-like aspects.

As your company contributes more to society and benefits the public interest, it will create a strong spiritual field like a religion and have a great impact on society. Although your company's main work may lie in business activities, you will be creating your own "believers," or people who have faith in your company's products. For example, there are many companies around the world that make children's toys. A company that earns a reputation for producing safe toys and making children happy will win people's faith in the company.

Creating dedicated followers

If you have managed to create a customer base that resembles the followers of a religion, it means you have gained repeat customers, which will stabilize your business. This applies to the hotel industry, too. To run a hotel or inn successfully, you need regular customers or fans. It will be difficult for a hotel or inn with only one-time customers to stay in business. They may come for the grand opening, but they will never return. Therefore, being able to attract repeaters is a requirement to succeed in the hotel industry.

People who manage a business must always think about creating repeat customers. Companies that have managed to earn people's trust, loyalty, or devotion will be stable in the long term and develop further.

3
The Spirit That Invites Prosperity

Personal happiness is connected to the happiness of society as a whole

Nowadays, many people seem to have forgotten about the spirit of service. They have forgotten the true nature of human beings and are living only to satisfy their selfish desires or egos. These people probably think they are just seeking happiness, but sadly, they are unaware that each person's happiness goes hand in hand with the happiness of society as a whole. This is why they look at life as though it is a competition over a piece of a pie. They think, "If I get a piece, there will be fewer pieces for others, but if others get a piece, there will be fewer for me. So, for me to be happy, I must take as many pieces of the pie as possible."

Here, I must say that they are only looking at one side of life without seeing the other. Society in this world is not a place where just one person can be happy. The happiness of the individual is closely linked to the happiness of society as a whole.

As more people live in service to others, it will create heaven on earth

It is the spirit of service that bridges your happiness and the happiness of others. While you live, you should always hope to be of service to others and the world, for this will lead to your own prosperity and, at the same time, the prosperity of society as a whole.

Another word for the spirit of service is love. Love expressed in the form of work is called service. But unfortunately, many people think of it as just another moral principle and do not take it seriously. As a result, they choose to live in a way that only benefits themselves and satisfies their selfish desires, which often leads them to clash with others and create unhappiness.

On the other hand, as more people live with the spirit of service and a wish to be helpful, however small their contribution to society may be, this world will naturally turn into heaven. This is the realization of prosperity itself.

The spirit of service is an essential element to achieve prosperity. Even if you are working on your own, you must have a sense of public duty. Always remind yourself that your work is closely connected to society as a whole and that doing good work will serve to make the world a better place.

The greatest happiness is that you, yourself, are happy, make those around you happy, and think that other people's happiness is your own happiness.

Words for Leaders 3
Great Ideas

"Look into someone's past,
And you will understand who they are."
These are the words of a master of life.

What, then, reveals a person's future?
Which of a person's qualities
Foretells their future?

The answer, I believe, is their ideas.
The driving force that shapes a person's future
Lies in their ideas.

What kind of ideas do you come up with
In times of suffering?

What kind of ideas do you come up with
In times of difficulty?
What do you think of
In times of sorrow?
What crosses your mind
When you see others happy?
What ideas come to mind
During the rising tide of your life?
And what do you think is the goal of your life?
What do you consider a great achievement in life?

Think of new ideas at each passing moment.
Confront new problems with new ideas.
Why must you think in the same way as others
Just because many people do?

What is now considered common sense
Started out as an idea thought up by an outstanding figure
Who acted upon it at a particular time in human history
And was followed by the people of later generations.

Come forth, new great figures.
Come forth, new common sense.
Revolutionary ideas are needed
To launch a spiritual revolution.
O people,
Let us come together and put forth great ideas.
You and me will surely be
The ones who carve out a new era.

Epilogue

Achieving True Success

Give many people your very best

It is not so difficult to achieve true success in this world. You can do so by living out your life while being one with the laws of the universe. The proof that you are living through your life with the laws of the universe is giving your very best to many people—in other words, offering them your very best.

When you give something to others, it may seem like you are losing what you give. However, according to the laws of the Spirit World, the more you give, the more abundant you will become. In fact, the more you give, the more you will be given—this is the law that governs the Spirit World. The same applies to success. If you live with the wish to always give your best to as many people as possible and to contribute to the happiness of many, your life will be blessed with the highest degree of success.

Therefore, live your life fully for the benefit of others and for the love of others, rather than basing your life on selfish motives. Aim to give your best to as many people as possible.

As you do, you will develop creativity and ingenuity. This is how you can achieve success.

First, you must understand that there can be no success without faith. You must also realize that the great universe is rich in and full of creative energy. This is the true nature of each of you as a child of Buddha or God. Given this nature, to invite abundant success, it is essential that you are very open-minded and live according to your innate Buddha-nature.

Keep your dreams alive and never stop challenging yourself

Pursue the kind of success that aligns with the Will of Buddha or God. If you wish strongly, it will surely materialize and manifest in this world. Hold on to that wish—it is important to keep holding it.

Visualize a clear image of success and engrave it deeply into your mind. Strongly wish that Buddha Land utopia will be realized on earth and that you will be someone who contributes to its realization as a strong leader. Always keep a clear image of yourself succeeding and continue to make diligent efforts. Do not forget to be creative and ingenious. Rather than complaining about your misfortune or being discouraged by failures or difficulties, bounce back again and again and take on new challenges. A strong will like this is needed.

Become a person full of motivation in the truest sense. Live in a way that your very existence motivates the people around you. This is the first step to making this world a brighter place.

Several sections in this book
are excerpts taken from the books by Ryuho Okawa:

PART I

Chapter 1

Section 2: *Introduction to Top Executive Management* (IRH Press, 2016)

Chapter 2

Section 1: *The Laws of Success* (IRH Press, 2017)

Section 2: *The Laws of Invincible Leadership* (IRH Press, 2018)

Chapter 3

Section 2: *Introduction to Top Executive Management* (IRH Press, 2016)

Section 3: *The Starting Point of Happiness* (IRH Press, 2017)

Chapter 4

Section 1: *Love, Nurture, and Forgive* (IRH Press, 2015)

Section 2: *The Laws of Hope* (IRH Press, 2020)

Section 3: *The Laws of Invincible Leadership* (IRH Press, 2018)

Chapter 5

Section 1: *Introduction to Top Executive Management* (IRH Press, 2016)

Section 3: *Best Selection of Ryuho Okawa's Early Lectures Volume 2: The Way to Human Perfection* (IRH Press, 2024)

PART II

Chapter 6

Section 1: *An Unshakable Mind* (IRH Press, 2023)

Section 3: *The Ten Principles from El Cantare Volume I* (IRH Press, 2021)

Chapter 7

Section 1: *Love, Nurture, and Forgive* (IRH Press, 2015)

Chapter 8

Section 1: *Invincible Thinking* (IRH Press, 2017)

Chapter 9

Section 1: *The Laws of Hope* (IRH Press, 2020)

Section 2: *The Laws of Success* (IRH Press, 2017)

Section 3: *The Laws of Invincible Leadership* (IRH Press, 2018)

PART III

Chapter 10

Section 1: *Introduction to Top Executive Management* (IRH Press, 2016)

Section 2: *The Laws of Hope* (IRH Press, 2020)

Section 3: *The Laws of Prosperity* (IRH Press, 2026)

Section 4: *The Laws of Success* (IRH Press, 2017)

Section 5: *Introduction to Top Executive Management* (IRH Press, 2016), *The Laws of Invincible Leadership* (IRH Press, 2018)

Chapter 11

Section 2: *The Laws of Hope* (IRH Press, 2020)

Section 3: *Introduction to Top Executive Management* (IRH Press, 2016)

Chapter 12

Section 1: *The Laws of Invincible Leadership* (IRH Press, 2018)

Section 3: *The Philosophy of Progress* (IRH Press, 2005)

Chapter 13

Section 1: *The Laws of Hope* (IRH Press, 2020)

Section 3: *The Laws of Prosperity* (IRH Press, 2026)

ABOUT THE AUTHOR

Founder and CEO of Happy Science Group.

Ryuho Okawa was born on July 7th, 1956, in Tokushima, Japan. After graduating from the University of Tokyo with a law degree, he joined a Tokyo-based trading company. While working at its New York headquarters, he studied international finance at the Graduate Center of the City University of New York. In 1981, he attained Great Enlightenment and became aware that he is El Cantare with a mission to bring salvation to all humankind.

In 1986, he established Happy Science. It now has members in 196 countries across the world, with more than 700 branches and temples, as well as 10,000 missionary houses around the world.

He has given over 3,500 lectures (of which more than 150 are in English) and published over 3,300 books (of which more than 600 are Spiritual Interview Series), and many are translated into 42 languages. Along with *The Laws of the Sun* and *The Laws of Hell*, many of the books have become best sellers or million sellers. To date, Happy Science has produced 29 movies under his supervision. He has given the original story and concept and is also the Executive Producer. He has also composed music and written lyrics for over 450 pieces.

Moreover, he is the Founder of Happy Science University and Happy Science Academy (Junior and Senior High School), Founder and President of the Happiness Realization Party, Founder and Honorary Headmaster of Happy Science Institute of Government and Management, Founder of IRH Press Co., Ltd., and the Chairperson of NEW STAR PRODUCTION Co., Ltd. and ARI Production Co., Ltd.

BOOKS BY RYUHO OKAWA

Related Books

THE LAWS OF SUCCESS

A SPIRITUAL GUIDE TO TURNING YOUR HOPES INTO REALITY

ISBN: 978-1-942125-15-0 • US$15.95

The Laws of Success offers 8 spiritual principles that will help us attain lasting success. The timeless wisdom and practical steps that Ryuho Okawa offers will serve as guiding principles for living a positive, constructive, and meaningful life.

THE ART OF INFLUENCE

28 WAYS TO WIN PEOPLE'S HEARTS AND BRING POSITIVE CHANGE TO YOUR LIFE

ISBN: 978-1-942125-48-8 • US$15.95

This is a compilation of 28 Q&A sessions. Inside are Okawa's deep wisdom that will offer you motivation and inspiration, and develop you into an influential leader with a big heart.

THINK BIG!

BE POSITIVE AND BE BRAVE TO ACHIEVE YOUR DREAMS

ISBN: 978-1-942125-04-4 • US$12.95

Think Big! offers the support and encouragement to shift to new ways of thinking and mastering self-discipline. The self-proven approach fosters stability and strength in the challenges we face.

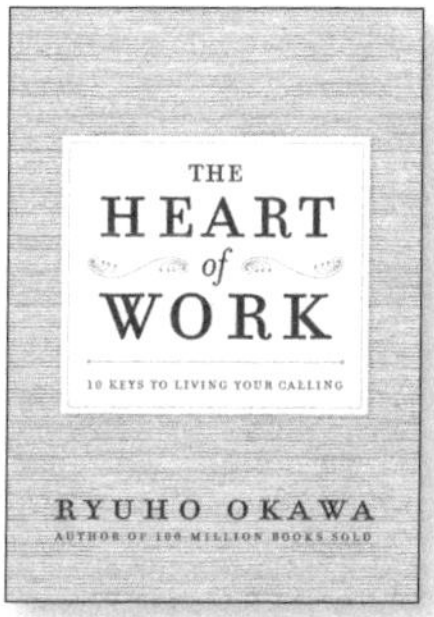

THE HEART OF WORK

10 KEYS TO LIVING YOUR CALLING

ISBN: 978-1-942125-03-7 • US$12.95

In this book, Ryuho Okawa introduces 10 key philosophies to live by to guide you through your work life. By grasping them, you can live your calling with utmost confidence and an unshakable mind.

THE LAWS OF HOPE

THE LIGHT IS HERE

ISBN:978-1-942125-76-1 • US$16.95

This book provides ways to bring light and hope to ourselves, even in the midst of sufferings and adversities. By making efforts in your current circumstances, you can fulfill your mission to shed light on yourself and those around you.

INVINCIBLE THINKING

AN ESSENTIAL GUIDE FOR A LIFETIME OF GROWTH, SUCCESS, AND TRIUMPH

ISBN: 978-1-942125-25-9 • US$16.95

This book introduces the principles of invincible thinking that will allow us to achieve long-lasting triumph. By learning from every experience and transforming it into wisdom, we will never be defeated.

FROM LOVE TO PRAYER

THE LIGHT OF HERMES DESCENDS ONCE AGAIN

ISBN: 978-1-958655-41-2 • US$17.95

This is an enlightening collection of poetic verses in the form of prayers that gently guides readers toward inner peace, spiritual awakening, and a deeper understanding of the true nature of love and prayer. Through these noble passages, readers will discover the truth of their souls.

THE CHALLENGE TO ESTABLISHING THE IMPERISHABLE TRUTH

NOW IS THE AGE OF SPIRITUAL AWAKENING

ISBN: 978-1-958655-39-9 • US$17.95

This book encourages readers to establish a spiritual view of life, understanding that life in this world is a soul-training ground for deepening love and enlightenment.

INVITATION TO FAITH

ATTAIN ENLIGHTENMENT AND GIVE LOVE

ISBN: 978-1-958655-71-9 • US$17.95

This world is not the only world there is, and life continues after death. The problems we face in life are actually chances for us to attain wisdom and cultivate selfless, pure love for others. This book presents the universal faith that people of today are seeking deep inside.

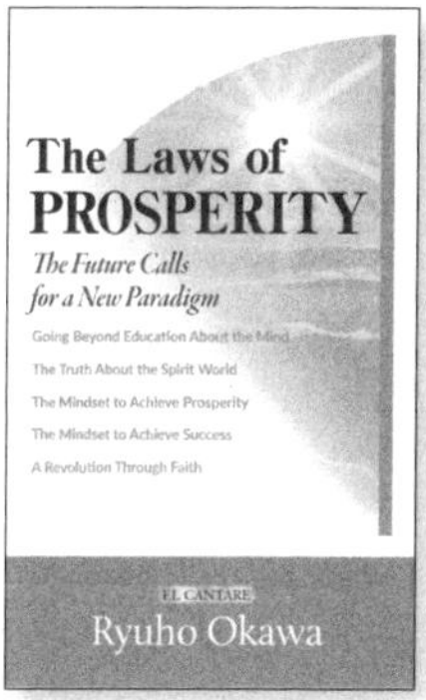

THE LAWS OF PROSPERITY

THE FUTURE CALLS FOR A NEW PARADIGM

ISBN: 978-4-8233-0478-1 • US$20.00

The Laws of Prosperity urges people to revolutionize their values in order to bring prosperity to Earth. It explores prosperity that extends from individuals to society and even the entire globe, the four good habits for a prosperous life, and how businesses and nations should address management crises.

Happiness

THE STARTING POINT OF HAPPINESS

AN INSPIRING GUIDE TO POSITIVE LIVING WITH FAITH, LOVE, AND COURAGE

ISBN: 978-1-942125-26-6 • US$16.95

This book is for those who are struggling to attain love and happiness. It reveals the simple mindsets that will help you overcome difficult circumstances and become happier.

THE LAWS OF HAPPINESS

LOVE, WISDOM, SELF-REFLECTION AND PROGRESS

ISBN: 978-1-942125-70-9 • US$16.95

Happiness is found within us, not outside. It is in how we think, view life, and work. This is an ultimate guide to becoming happy through the Fourfold Path of Love, Wisdom, Self-Reflection, and Progress—the universal law of happiness.

BE INFINITELY KIND

FOR WE ARE LIVING IN THE GREAT RIVER OF LOVE

ISBN: 978-1-958655-27-6 • US$17.95

In this book, Ryuho Okawa invites readers to explore the deeper spiritual virtues of love and kindness—essential qualities for building strong, lasting relationships with those we hold dear. Truthfully, the more love we give, the wealthier our souls become.

WORRY-FREE LIVING

LET GO OF STRESS AND LIVE IN PEACE AND HAPPINESS

ISBN: 978-1-942125-51-8 • US$16.95

This is a guide for those who are overwhelmed by the stress that comes with living. It will help you change how you look at and approach life's worries and problems for the better.

AN UNSHAKABLE MIND

HOW TO OVERCOME LIFE'S DIFFICULTIES

ISBN: 978-1-942125-91-4 • US$17.95

This book will guide you to build the genuine self-confidence necessary to shape a resilient character and withstand life's turbulence. Ryuho Okawa breaks down the causes of life's difficulties and provides solutions to overcome them.

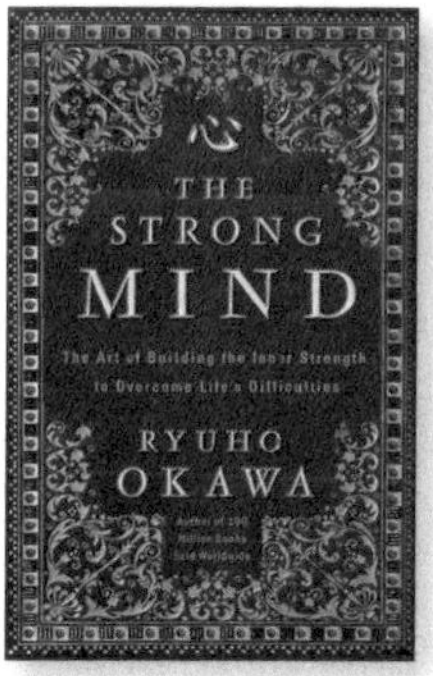

THE STRONG MIND

THE ART OF BUILDING THE INNER STRENGTH TO OVERCOME LIFE'S DIFFICULTIES

ISBN: 978-1-942125-36-5 • US$15.95

This book will inspire and empower you to take courage, develop a cultivated heart, and achieve resilience and hardiness so that you can break through your limits and keep winning in the battle of your life.

The Laws of the Sun

One Source, One Planet, One People

ISBN: 978-1-942125-43-3 • US$15.95

How was this world created, and why do humans live in this world? *The Laws of the Sun* answers life's questions humans have always had throughout history. In this book, Ryuho Okawa outlines the laws that govern the universe and provides a road map for living one's life with greater purpose and meaning. The Truth taught in this book will significantly transform your life and allow you to develop love and acceptance toward people of all races and religions.

The Laws of Eternity

El Cantare Unveils the Structure of the Spirit World

ISBN: 978-1-958655-16-0 • US$17.95

Where do we come from, and where do we go after death? *The Laws of Eternity* answers life's most important questions that we are all confronted with at some point or another. Author Ryuho Okawa takes us on a journey to the other world, a place where we came from before we were born and return to after death. Open its pages and discover the eternal mysteries and the ultimate secrets of Earth's spirit group that have been covered by the veil of legends and myths.

Basic Teachings of Happy Science

The Ten Principles from El Cantare Volume I

Ryuho Okawa's First Lectures on His Basic Teachings

ISBN: 978-1-942125-85-3 • US$16.95

How did Happy Science begin? What are its teachings? What is its aim? This is a compilation of early lectures that built the foundation of Happy Science.

The Ten Principles from El Cantare Volume II

Ryuho Okawa's First Lectures on His Wish to Save the World

ISBN: 978-1-942125-86-0 • US$16.95

In *Volume II*, Ryuho Okawa's passionate messages for realizing a utopia on earth reveal the Truth about God's three major inventions, the mission of religion, and more.

What Is Happy Science?

Best Selection of Ryuho Okawa's Early Lectures (Volume 1)

ISBN: 978-1-942125-99-0 • US$17.95

Volume 1 of the Best Selection series teaches the eternal Truth, including the secret of the mind, the true meaning of love, and how to end hatred and world conflicts.

The Way to Human Perfection

Best Selection of Ryuho Okawa's Early Lectures (Volume 2)

ISBN: 978-1-958655-20-7 • US$17.95

The path to enlightenment starts from understanding "the eternal viewpoint of life." By recognizing that we have eternal life, we can realize that caring and bringing joy to others are the keys to true happiness and success.

Health & Wellness

HEALING FROM WITHIN

LIFE-CHANGING KEYS TO CALM, SPIRITUAL, AND HEALTHY LIVING

ISBN:978-1-942125-18-1 • US$15.95

In this book, Ryuho Okawa reveals the true causes and remedies for various illnesses that modern medicine cannot heal. You will learn about the relationship between mind and body.

THE MIRACLE POWER TO OVERCOME ILLNESS

HEALING THROUGH FAITH

ISBN: 978-1-958655-17-7 • US$17.95

The truth inside this book will take you beyond the worldly understanding of illness and help you awaken to the power of faith. Learn to become a person who can receive the miracle power from heaven.

WORDS TO READ IN TIMES OF ILLNESS

ISBN: 978-1-958655-07-8 • US$17.95

Ryuho Okawa has written 100 Healing Messages to comfort the souls of those going through illness. A time of illness is an ideal time for us to contemplate recent and past events, as well as our relationship with the people around us.

Enlightenment

THE ESSENCE OF BUDDHA

THE PATH TO ENLIGHTENMENT

ISBN: 978-1-942125-06-8 • US$14.95

The essence of Shakyamuni Buddha's original teachings of the mind is explained in simple words. Through this book, you will learn how to attain inner happiness, the wisdom to conquer ego, and to enter the path to enlightenment.

THE LAWS OF GREAT ENLIGHTENMENT

ALWAYS WALK WITH BUDDHA

ISBN: 978-1-942125-62-4 • US$17.95

Discover the power of forgiveness from Buddha's enlightenment and compassion, and the true relationship of work and enlightenment. In addition, the author reveals his own experience when he attained Great Enlightenment.

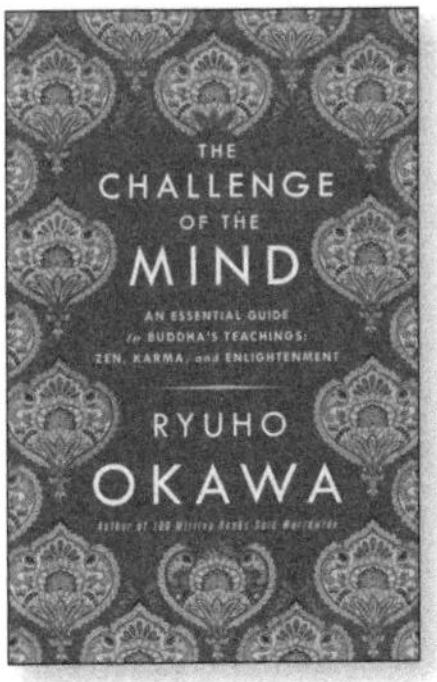

THE CHALLENGE OF THE MIND

AN ESSENTIAL GUIDE TO BUDDHA'S TEACHINGS: ZEN, KARMA, AND ENLIGHTENMENT

ISBN: 978-1-942125-45-7 • US$16.95

In this book, Ryuho Okawa explains essential Buddhist tenets and how to put them into practice. He offers a solid basis of reason and an intellectual understanding of Buddhist concepts.

Enlightenment

THE CHALLENGE OF ENLIGHTENMENT

NOW, HERE, THE NEW DHARMA WHEEL TURNS

ISBN: 978-1-942125-92-1 • US$17.95

What is the role of enlightenment in facing the challenges of the modern world? By reading this book, your mind learns to savor inner peace, and you will be empowered to make profound life improvements.

THE REBIRTH OF BUDDHA

MY ETERNAL DISCIPLES, HEAR MY WORDS

ISBN: 978-1-942125-95-2 • US$17.95

These are the messages of Buddha, who has returned to this modern age as promised to his eternal beloved disciples. They are in simple words and poetic style, yet contain profound messages.

THE ETERNAL BUDDHA

NOW, HERE, IS THE IMPERISHABLE LIGHT

ISBN: 978-1-958655-19-1 • US$17.95

Embedded in this book is a message from Eternal Buddha, the parent of your soul. You will discover the true origin of your soul and why you have chosen to be born in this time.

THE DESCENT OF JAPANESE FATHER GOD AME-NO-MIOYA-GAMI

THE "GOD OF CREATION" IN THE ANCIENT DOCUMENT *HOTSUMA TSUTAE*

ISBN: 978-1-943928-35-4 • US$14.95

Nearly 30,000 years ago, Ame-no-Mioya-Gami descended on the foothills of Mt. Fuji. By reading this book, you can find the origin of the Japanese spirit and understand how the ancient Japanese civilization influenced other countries.

TRUE BUSHIDO SPOKEN BY AME-NO-MIOYA-GAMI

THE JAPANESE FATHER GOD TEACHES HOW WE SHOULD LIVE AND DIE

ISBN: 978-4823304-60-6 • US$20.00

Standing at the origin of Japanese civilization, Ame-no-Mioya-Gami reveals the core spirit of Bushido: 'The view of death and justice,' 'Why selflessness is essential to achieving justice,' 'The act of seppuku is not sacred in itself—it's the spirit behind it that matters.'

Spiritual Truth

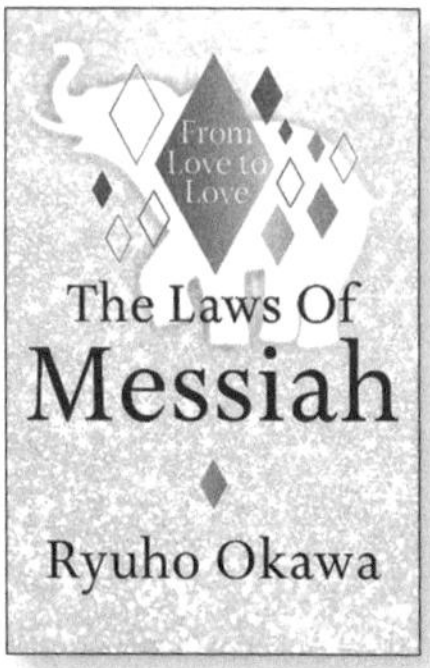

THE LAWS OF MESSIAH

FROM LOVE TO LOVE

ISBN: 978-1-942125-90-7 • US$16.95

"What is Messiah?" This book carries an important message of love and guidance to people living now from the Modern-Day Messiah or the Modern-Day Savior. It also reveals the secret of Shambhala, the spiritual center of Earth.

THE LAWS OF HELL

"IT" FOLLOWS.....

ISBN: 978-1-958655-04-7 • US$17.95

Whether you believe it or not, the Spirit World and hell do exist, and unfortunately, 1 in 2 people are falling into hell. To stop hell from spreading and to save the souls of all human beings, Ryuho Okawa has compiled vital teachings in this book.

THE LAWS OF SECRET

AWAKEN TO THIS NEW WORLD AND CHANGE YOUR LIFE

ISBN:978-1-942125-81-5 • US$16.95

This book reveals how our lives are affected by invisible influences, including the spiritual reasons behind influenza, the novel coronavirus infection, and other illnesses. Discover the spiritual view of life that will help you refine your soul.

THE MYSTICAL LAWS

GOING BEYOND THE DIMENSIONAL BOUNDARIES

ISBN: 979-8-887370-3-85 • US$14.95

"Within an hour of reading this book, all that you have accepted as common knowledge will crumble away. Indeed, no school or mass media has ever taught you the truth. Whatever doubts you may have, this book will reveal the truths of the great universe." —From Preface

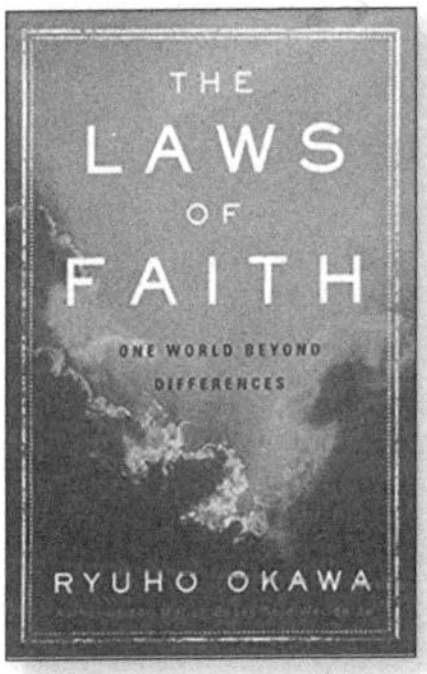

THE LAWS OF FAITH

ONE WORLD BEYOND DIFFERENCES

ISBN: 978-1-942125-34-1 • US$15.95

Ryuho Okawa preaches the core teachings of the world religion and the faith in the God of Earth. Through this book, you will learn to go beyond different values, harmonize with each other and between nations, and create a world filled with peace and prosperity.

THE LAWS OF BRONZE

LOVE ONE ANOTHER, BECOME ONE PEOPLE

ISBN: 978-1-942125-50-1 • US$15.95

This book will show people from all walks of life that they can solve their problems by finding faith and practicing love. When all of us on this planet discover our common spiritual origin revealed in this book, we can truly love one another and become one people on Earth.

Books for the Coming Space Age

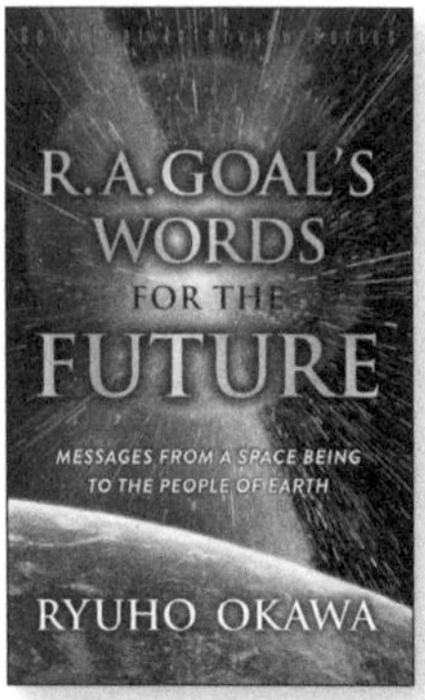

R. A. Goal's Words for the Future

Messages from a Space Being to the People of Earth

ISBN: 979-8-887370-52-1 • US$11.95

R. A. Goal is a certified messiah from Planet Andalucia Beta in Ursa Minor, who protects and guides us. By reading this book, you will have a clear picture of how the world now needs true leaders who can think about world justice.

Spiritual Messages from Yaidron

Save the World from Destruction

ISBN: 978-1-943928-23-1 • US$11.95

Yaidron is a certified messiah from Planet Elder in the Magellanic Clouds. In this book, he explains what was occurring behind the coup in Myanmar and the Taliban's control over Afghanistan, and warns of the imminent danger approaching Taiwan.

Spiritual Messages from Metatron

Light in the Times of Crisis

ISBN: 978-1-943928-19-4 • US$11.95

Metatron, a certified messiah from Planet Include in Sagittarius, has sent a message upon seeing the crisis of Earth. You will learn the real intention of China and the danger of Japan's appeasement policy toward China.

Secrets of Future Science

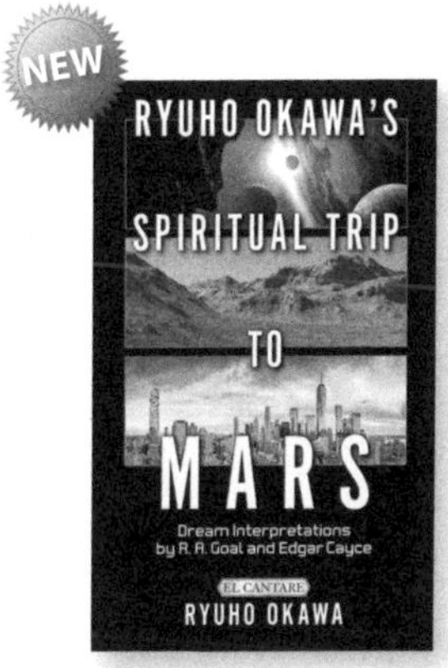

RYUHO OKAWA'S SPIRITUAL TRIP TO MARS

DREAM INTERPRETATIONS BY R. A. GOAL AND EDGAR CAYCE

ISBN: 978-4-8233-0481-1 • US$20.00

In this book, R.A. Goal and the spirit of Edgar Cayce interpret Master Okawa's dreams. Is there life on Mars? Will we find a new energy source in the 2070s? Read and find out.

KANJIZAI, BUDDHA'S OMNISCIENT POWER OF PERCEPTION

GOING BEYOND TIME, SPACE, AND THE GREAT UNIVERSE

ISBN: 978-1958655-29-0 • US$17.95

This book unveils what it means to possess real spiritual power—one that inspires humility, sincerity, and the pursuit of genuine enlightenment.

THE TRUTH ABOUT EARTH, THE UNIVERSE, THE SPIRIT WORLD

LIFE'S Q&A WITH EL CANTARE

ISBN: 978-1-958655-26-9 • US$17.95

A compilation of 28 Q&A sessions by Ryuho Okawa, where he answers numerous intricate questions varying from the theory of evolution to the creation of the multidimensional universe, all without a script.

WHO IS EL CANTARE?

El Cantare means "the Light of the Earth." He is the Supreme God of the Earth who has been guiding humankind since the beginning of Genesis, and He is the Creator of the universe. He is whom Jesus called Father and Muhammad called Allah, and He is *Ame-no-Mioya-Gami*, the Japanese Father God. He is also known as Vishnu in India and Tiandi in China. Different parts of El Cantare's core consciousness have descended to Earth in the past, once as Alpha and another as Elohim. His branch spirits, such as Shakyamuni Buddha and Hermes, have descended to Earth many times and helped to flourish many civilizations. To build a new civilization on Earth by uniting various religions and integrating various fields of study, a part of the core consciousness has now descended as Master Ryuho Okawa.

Alpha is a part of the core consciousness of El Cantare, who descended to Earth around 330 million years ago. Alpha preached Earth's Truth to harmonize and unify Earth-born humans and space people who came from other planets.

Elohim is a part of the core consciousness of El Cantare, who descended to Earth around 150 million years ago. He gave wisdom, mainly on the differences between light and darkness, good and evil.

Ame-no-Mioya-Gami (Japanese Father God) is a Being who is close to the core consciousness of Lord El Cantare, and is the Creator God and the Father God who appears in ancient literature, *Hotsuma Tsutae*. It is believed that He descended on the foothills of Mt. Fuji about 30,000 years ago and built the Fuji dynasty, which is the root of the Japanese civilization. Ame-no-Mioya-Gami's Teachings spread to ancient civilizations of other countries in the world.

EL CANTARE'S BRANCH SPIRITS

Shakyamuni Buddha was born in Nepal around 2,600 years ago as the prince of the Shakya clan. When he was 29 years old, he renounced the world and sought enlightenment. He later attained Great Enlightenment and spent most of his life in India teaching and practicing the Truth. He is the founder of Buddhism, which has spread extensively throughout Asia.

Hermes is one of the 12 Olympian gods in Greek mythology, but the spiritual Truth is that he taught the teachings of love and progress around 4,300 years ago, which became the origin of the current Western civilization. He is a hero who truly existed.

Ophealis was born in Greece around 6,500 years ago and was the leader who went on an expedition as far as Egypt. He is the God of miracles, prosperity, and arts, and is known as Osiris in Egyptian mythology.

Rient Arl Croud was born as a king of the ancient Incan Empire around 7,000 years ago and taught about the mysteries of the mind. In the heavenly world, he is responsible for the interactions that take place between Earth and various planets.

Thoth was an almighty leader who built the golden age of the Atlantis civilization around 12,000 years ago. In Egyptian mythology, he is known as God Thoth.

Ra Mu was a leader who built the golden age of the civilization of Mu around 17,000 years ago. As a religious leader and a politician, he ruled by uniting religion and politics.

ABOUT HAPPY SCIENCE

Happy Science is a religious group founded on the faith in El Cantare, who is the God of the Earth and the Creator of the universe. The true essence of human beings is an eternal soul created by God, and we go through the cycle of reincarnation to train and develop our souls. We have been carrying out various activities to spread this spiritual value and build a peaceful and prosperous world that God wishes. At Happy Science, we explore righteousness, in other words, God's Will. This is called the "Exploration of Right Mind." More specifically, it means to practice the Fourfold Path: Love, Wisdom, Self-Reflection, and Progress. This is the path that leads humans to attain happiness that carries over from this world to the next.

Love–practicing "love that gives"
To give love to others without expecting anything in return is the starting point of happiness. By practicing "love that gives," you will become closer to God.

Wisdom—studying spiritual truth
By studying the Truth, you will be able to distinguish good and evil, live righteously, and learn the heart of God. True wisdom leads people to true happiness.

Self-Reflection—correcting your mistakes
Self-reflection is the act of correcting wrongful thoughts and actions you have accumulated during the day and regaining the pure, true nature of the soul.

Progress—creating utopia on earth
True progress is about spreading happiness to others and improving society as you achieve your own success. This will create utopia on earth.

PLACES OF WORSHIP FOR HAPPY SCIENCE

Shoja

—A PLACE TO REFINE YOUR MIND,
GAIN SPIRITUAL WISDOM, AND BE REBORN

Happy Science shoja (temple) is a sacred spiritual field where you can deepen your faith and heighten your enlightenment. Under the spiritual guidance of high spirits, shoja holds various seminars to improve individual character and ritual prayers to help believers solve their life problems and make progress. By participating in them, you can regain the peaceful and blissful mind that you may have lost in your everyday life.

29 SHOJAS IN JAPAN, 3 SHOJAS AND LA DOJO OVERSEAS

San Francisco

Local Branch

—A PLACE TO CHANGE YOUR DESTINY

Since 1986, Happy Science has been carrying out various activities to produce people who can truly say, "I am happy." At our local branches, many new believers are being born and are leading better lives through faith in Lord God El Cantare. All kinds of events take place here, such as lecture viewing, book seminars, prayers, and counseling sessions. Everyone is welcome!

HAPPY SCIENCE'S ENGLISH SUTRA

"The True Words Spoken By Buddha"

"The True Words Spoken By Buddha" is an English sutra given directly from the spirit of Shakyamuni Buddha, who is a part of Master Ryuho Okawa's subconscious. The words in this sutra are not of a mere human being but are the words of God or Buddha sent directly from the ninth dimension, which is the highest realm of the Earth's Spirit World.

"The True Words Spoken By Buddha" is an essential sutra for us to connect and live with God or Buddha's Will as our own.

MEMBERSHIPS

MEMBERSHIP

If you would like to know more about Happy Science, please consider becoming a member. Those who pledge to believe in Lord El Cantare and wish to learn more can join us.

When you become a member, you will receive the following sutras: "The True Words Spoken By Buddha," "Prayer to the Lord," and "Prayer to Guardian and Guiding Spirits."

DEVOTEE MEMBER

If you would like to learn the teachings of Happy Science and walk the path of faith, become a Devotee member who pledges devotion to the Three Treasures, which are Buddha, Dharma, and Sangha. Buddha refers to Lord El Cantare, Master Ryuho Okawa. Dharma refers to Master Ryuho Okawa's teachings. Sangha refers to Happy Science. Devoting to the Three Treasures will let your Buddha nature shine, and you will enter the path to attain true freedom of the mind.

Becoming a devotee means you become Buddha's disciple. You will discipline your mind and act to bring happiness to society.

EMAIL OR **PHONE CALL**

Please turn to the contact information page.

ONLINE member.happy-science.org/signup/

CONTACT INFORMATION

Happy Science is a worldwide organization with branches and temples around the globe. For full details, visit happy-science.org. The following are some of our main Happy Science locations:

UNITED STATES AND CANADA

New York
79 Franklin St., New York, NY 10013, USA
Call/Text: 1-929-323-4737
Email: ny@happy-science.org
Website: happyscience-usa.org

New Jersey
66 Hudson St., #2R, Hoboken, NJ 07030, USA
Call/Text: 1-929-323-4737
Email: nj@happy-science.org
Website: happyscience-usa.org

Chicago
33 West Higgins Rd. 4040,
South Barrington, IL 60010, USA
Phone: 1-630-937-3077
Email: chicago@happy-science.org
Website: happyscience-usa.org

Florida
5208 8th St., Zephyrhills, FL 33542, USA
Phone: 1-813-715-0000
Fax: 1-813-715-0010
Email: florida@happy-science.org
Website: happyscience-usa.org

Atlanta
Phone: 1-813-715-0000
Email: atlanta@happy-science.org

San Francisco
525 Clinton St.
Redwood City, CA 94062, USA
Phone & Fax: 1-650-363-2777
Email: sf@happy-science.org
Website: happyscience-usa.org

Los Angeles
1590 E. Del Mar Blvd., Pasadena,
CA 91106, USA
Call/Text: 1-626-788-8770
Email: la@happy-science.org
Website: happyscience-usa.org

Orange County
16541 Gothard St. Suite 104
Huntington Beach, CA 92647
Phone: 1-714-659-1501
Email: oc@happy-science.org
Website: happyscience-usa.org

San Diego
Call/Text: 1-619-374-7880

Hawaii
Phone: 1-808-591-9772
Fax: 1-808-591-9776
Email: hi@happy-science.org
Website: happyscience-usa.org

Kauai
3343 Kanakolu Street, Suite 5
Lihue, HI 96766, USA
Phone: 1-808-822-7007
Fax: 1-808-822-6007
Email: kauai-hi@happy-science.org
Website: happyscience-usa.org

Toronto
845 The Queensway
Etobicoke, ON, M8Z 1N6, Canada
Call/Text: 1-647-494-7779
Email: toronto@happy-science.org
Website: happy-science.ca

Vancouver
#201-2607 East 49th Avenue,
Vancouver, BC, V5S 1J9, Canada
Phone: 1-604-437-7735
Fax: 1-604-437-7764
Email: vancouver@happy-science.org
Website: happy-science.ca